London for Free

Also in this series:

Europe for Free
by Brian Butler

Hawaii for Free
by Frances Carter

DC for Free
by Brian Butler

Paris for Free
(Or Extremely Cheap)
by Mark Beffart

The Southwest for Free
by Greg & Mary Jane Edwards

3rd REVISED EDITION

LONDON
FOR FREE

Hundreds of Free Things to Do in London

BRIAN BUTLER

Mustang Publishing
Memphis, TN

Library of Congress Cataloging-in-Publication Data
Butler, Brian, 1950-
    London for free : hundreds of free things to do in London /
Brian Butler. -- 3rd rev. ed.
        p.   cm.
    ISBN 0-914457-86-1
    1. London (England) -- Guide-books. I. Title.
DA679.B87   1997
914.2104'859--dc21   96-49222
                                                            CIP

Printed on acid-free paper.
10 9 8 7 6 5 4 3 2

*This book is dedicated to Steve:
forever free, forever young,
forever in our hearts.*

Acknowledgments

I would like to express my sincere gratitude to the following individuals and institutions for their help in making this book possible: Susan C. Williams of the London Tourist Board; Lena Martinez of the Tower Hamlets Information Centre; Sonia Mullins and Al Hanagan from the Lambeth Public Relations Office; Sylvia Chant, Islington Council Tourism Officer; Marleen Francis of London Regional Transport; Borough of Kensington and Chelsea Information Office; Greenwich Tourist Information Centre; Clerkenwell Heritage Centre; City of Westminster Information Office; British Travel Centre, Regent Street; Hackney Information Bureau; and the Docklands Light Railway Information Centre.

Brian Butler

Contents

Introduction

LONDON IS RENOWNED for its great museums, regal palaces, festive ceremonies, and enduring landmarks, but few of the millions of annual visitors to Britain's capital realize that hundreds of the city's best attractions and events are absolutely *free*.

Whether this is your first or your twenty-first visit to London, *London for Free* will help you discover treasures of British heritage, priceless works of art, pageants rich in color and history, renowned museums, exciting festivals, showcases of modern technology, architectural gems, behind-the-scenes tours, concerts, zoos, palatial mansions, avant-garde galleries, quirky collections, stunning gardens, national shrines, and much, much more. And it's all free!

Using This Book

London is a gargantuan metropolis, sprawling over 650 square miles of town and suburb. Exploring this far-flung city can be confusing and tiring without organization and planning. To that end, we divided *London for Free* geographically by borough, village, and neighborhood. Entries are also grouped by the all-important **postal code prefix**. Included in all London street addresses and on most street signs, the postal code provides an essential reference when navigating the city.

Each entry supplies germane background information on the attraction, along with the street address, phone number (where applicable), and admission days and hours. Codes (listed below) indicate the nearest Underground station and bus routes, sites with hassle-free access for people with limited mobility, entries that children will enjoy, and attractions that offer free tours.

Things Change

A simple caveat before you begin: Although we have made every effort to ensure accuracy, please remember that admission policies and opening hours will change, and some attractions that were free at press time may now charge a fee or request a donation.

We welcome your comments or suggestions for future editions of this book. Write to *London for Free*, c/o Mustang Publishing, P.O. Box 3004, Memphis, TN 38173, U.S.A.

KEY

B   **Bus routes**

C   **Appealing to children**

H   **Handicapped accessible**

T   **Tours offered**

U   **Nearby Underground stations**

Getting Around

GREATER LONDON BOASTS probably the finest public transportation system in Europe. If you take the time to learn the system and plan your route in advance, traveling around London will be surprisingly easy.

London Regional Transport (LRT) operates both the buses and the subway system within the 650 square miles of Greater London. LRT maintains a 24-hour telephone information service at 0171-222-1234, providing information on schedules, routes, and fares for LRT buses, the Underground, and the train lines run by British Rail in the London area. Also, LRT Travel Information Centres provide free maps, leaflets, timetables, and helpful pointers for getting the most out of London's public transit system.

Bus and Underground fares are based on a system of six zones. A short trip crossing several zones can cost more than a long haul within one zone. The most economical way to get around is to purchase one of LRT's passes, valid for unlimited travel and available by the day, week, or month. The best buy is the **Travelcard**, good on the entire bus and Underground system, the Docklands Light Railway (DLR), and British Rail's Network Southeast lines. In North America, travel agents and British Rail offices sell Travelcards for three, four, or seven days. If you plan to purchase a pass for a longer duration in London, bring a passport-sized photograph and buy the pass at any Underground station (including Heathrow terminals).

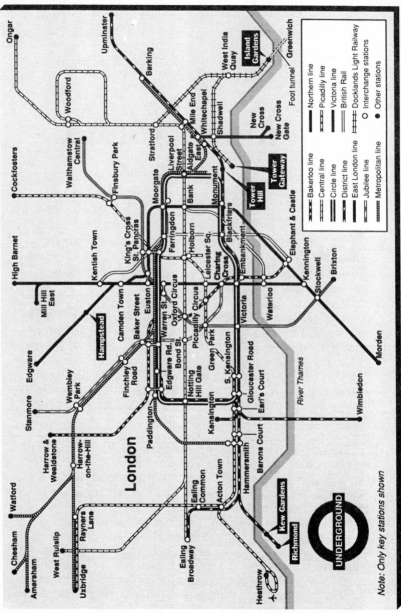

Note: Only key stations shown

UNDERGROUND

Bakerloo line
Central line
Circle line
District line
East London line
Jubilee line
Metropolitan line
Northern line
Picadilly line
Victoria line
British Rail
Docklands Light Railway
○ Interchange stations
● Other stations
Foot tunnel

The Underground

London has the oldest, deepest, and most extensive subway system in the world. Nearly three million passengers a day travel through "The Tube's" network of 248 stations.

If you don't have a Travelcard, you can purchase tickets from self-service machines in most stations or from the station ticket office. To enter the station, put your ticket through the automatic gate or show it as you pass by the barrier. You must keep your ticket until you've passed the barriers at your destination, so remember to take your ticket back from the machine. There are hefty fines for using the Underground without a valid ticket.

Underground trains run every few minutes from 5:30am to midnight Monday-Saturday and from 7:30am to 11:30pm on Sunday. Overcrowding is common at rush hours (8:00am-9:30am and 4:45pm-6:30pm), so try to travel other than peak times.

A note of caution: While crime in the London Underground is not nearly as serious as in New York subways, theft and harassment are on the rise.

Buses

Though London's double-decker buses are the best way to see the sights while getting around, they are subject to seemingly endless delays in the gridlocked traffic. There are 570 bus routes throughout Greater London. Buses operate from 5:30am to midnight, and there's a limited night service on 34 routes from 11:00pm to 6:00am.

Buses will stop automatically only at stops designated by the LRT symbol, a red horizontal line bisecting a red circle on a white background. Buses will stop at "red request stops" only if you raise your arm to hail the driver. Route numbers are posted on signs at the bus stops, and framed timetables List the places served.

Buses use a zone fare system similar to the Underground's. On newer, single-deck buses, you must have correct change or a transit pass to board. On double-deckers, there's usually a conductor who will collect fares or check passes; otherwise, pay the driver or show your pass as you board. To get off, ring the bell before the bus reaches your stop.

British Rail
British Rail is also known as BritRail or just BR. Its Network Southeast lines crisscross Greater London. All routes intersect with at least one major Underground line for convenient transfers. LRT Travelcards are valid on BR lines throughout Greater London.

Taxis
London's black taxis are nearly as famous as its red double-decker buses. You can hail a cab on the street when its yellow "For Hire" sign is lit. You can also order a taxi by phone, but be prepared to pay extra for being picked up. The largest company is **Radio Taxis** with a 2,500-car fleet. Book by phoning 0171-286-0286, 272-3030, or 272-0272 any time.

You can be charged only the amount shown on the taxi's meter. (A fare table is on the back of the driver's seat.) However, the meter will automatically add a fee of one pound, and additional charges will be levied for extra passengers and luggage. A 10-15% tip is voluntary but expected.

Cars
Don't bother. Park it and take public transportation!

River Boats
Riverbus operates a fast, efficient riverboat system Linking Chelsea, Greenwich, and the Docklands, with stops at South Bank, Victoria Embankment, the City, and London Bridge. The scheduled weekday service runs every 20 minutes from 7:00am to 10:00pm; weekend service operates 10:00am-6:00pm, with catamarans every half-hour. The fare for the entire trip from Chelsea to Greenwich is three pounds; short journeys are one pound. The Riverbus is a great way to beat the traffic, with the added bonus of some of London's finest views.

Airports

Heathrow Airport is accessible on the Piccadilly Underground line, which connects all airport terminals and runs to Central London (a 45-minute trip) for £3.20 (free with a Travelcard). Trains run from Heathrow Monday-Saturday every five minutes from 5:08am-11:49pm and Sunday from 6:00am-10:43pm. Trains depart Piccadilly Circus for Heathrow Monday-Saturday 5:45am-12:21pm and Sunday 7:00am-11:36pm.

Airbus #A1 runs from Grosvenor Gardens, SW1 daily from 6:00am-10:00pm for £4.00 one-way or £6.00 roundtrip. Airbus #A2 runs on the same schedule (every 30 minutes) from Euston Bus Station and Woburn Place, WC1. Green Line's "Flightline" buses link Victoria Bus Station and Heathrow with hourly service from 6:15am-6:30pm for £7.50 one-way or £11.00 roundtrip.

Fast and frequent British Rail service links Gatwick Airport and Victoria Station every 15 minutes from 5:30am-midnight and every 30 minutes from midnight-5:00am for £9.00.

Maps

The best investment any visitor to London can make (after a copy of *London for Free,* of course) is a good map of the city or a pocket atlas. For a free map, write the British Tourist Authority in New York, Chicago, Los Angeles, or Toronto (addresses on page 18) and request their "London Map."

Information Sources

London Tourist Board Centres

Harrods, Brompton Road, SW1 (phone 0171-730-1234). Open Mon-Sat 9:30am-6:00pm.

Heathrow Terminals 1, 2, 3 — Underground Station concourse. Open daily, 9:00am- 6:00pm.

Heathrow Terminal 2 — Arrivals concourse. Open daily, 9:00am-6:00pm.

Selfridges, Oxford St., W1 (phone 0171-629-1234). Open Mon-Sat 9:30am-6:00pm.

Tower of London, West Gate, EC3. Open April-Oct daily, 10:00am-6:00pm.

Victoria Station Forecourt, SW1 (phone 0171-730-3488). *April-Oct:* open daily, 8:00am-7:00pm; *Nov 6-April 4:* open Mon-Sat 9:00am-7:00pm, Sun 9:00am-5:00pm.

Other Tourist Information Centres

Bloomsbury, 35 Woburn Place, WC1 (phone 0171-580-4599). Open daily, 7:30am-7:30pm.

British Travel Centre, 12 Regent St., SW1 (phone 0171-730-3400). Open Mon-Fri 9:00am-6:30pm, Sat 9:00am-5:00pm, Sun 10:00am-4:00pm.

Camden, 100 Euston Rd., NW1 (phone 0171-278-4444). Open Mon-Sat 10:00am-5:00pm.

City of London, St. Paul's Churchyard, EC4 (phone 0171-606-3030). Open daily, 9:30am-5:00pm.

Clerkenwell Heritage Centre, 35 St. John's Square, EC1 (phone 0171-250-1039). Open Mon-Fri 10:00am-5:00pm.

Greenwich, 46 Church St., SE10 (phone 0181-858-6376). Open daily, 10:00am-5:00pm.

Hackney, Mare St., E8 (phone 0181-986-3123). Open Mon-Fri 9:00am-5:00pm.

Islington, 44 Duncan St., N1 (phone 0171-278-8787). Open Tues-Sat 10:00am-5:00pm.

Kensington and Chelsea, Hornton St., W8 (phone 0171-937-5464). Open Mon-Fri 9:00am-5:00pm.

Lambeth, Brixton Hill, SW2 (phone 0171-274-7722). Open Mon-Fri 9:00am-4:00pm.

Richmond, Whittaker Ave. (phone 0181-940-9125). Open Mon-Sat 10:00am-5:00pm.

Tower Hamlets, Cambridge Heath Rd., E2 (phone 0181-980-4831). Open Mon-Fri 9:00am-5:00pm.

Twickenham, Garfield Rd. (phone 0181-892-0032). Open Mon-Sat 10:00am-5:00pm.

Westminster, Victoria St., SW1 (phone 0171-828-8070). Open Mon-Fri 9:00am-4:00pm.

London Transport Information Centres

Euston Underground Station. Open daily, 7:30am-6:00pm.

Heathrow Arrivals Terminals. Open Mon-Fri 7:15am-10:00pm, Sat & Sun 8:15am-9:00pm.

King's Cross Underground. Open daily, 8:15am-6:00pm.

Oxford Circus Underground. Open Mon-Sat 8:15am-6:00pm.

Piccadilly Circus Underground. Open daily, 8:15am-6:00pm.

Victoria Station. Open daily, 8:15am-9:30pm.

24-Hour Bus Information: phone 0171-222-1234.

24-Hour British Rail Information: phone 0171-928-5100.

British Tourist Authority
Offices in North America

551 Fifth Ave.
New York, NY 10036
phone 212-986-2200

625 N. Michigan Ave.
Chicago, IL 60611
phone 312-787-0490

350 South Figueroa St.
Los Angeles, CA 90071
phone 213-628-3525

2305 Cedar Springs Rd.
Dallas, TX 75201
phone 214-720-4040

94 Cumberland St.
Toronto, Ontario
M5R 3N3 Canada
phone 416-925-6326

CENTRAL
LONDON

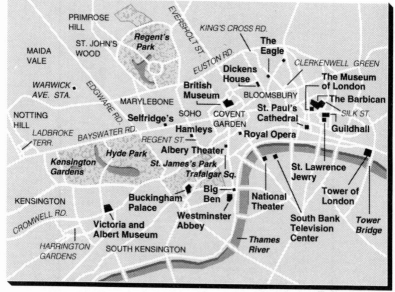

*Sir, when a man is tired of London,
he is tired of life; for there is in
London all that life can afford.*

Samuel Johnson (1709-84)

Central London

The City, Holborn, and Clerkenwell

Museum of London
The Museum of London, one of the city's most entertaining museums, is devoted entirely to London and its people. Everything on view portrays some aspect of the 2,000-year history of this great city. Imaginative, prize-winning displays include reconstructions of a Roman household, a 17th-century merchant's home, Victorian shops, and a grim Newgate Prison cell. Don't miss the extraordinary Lord Mayor's Ceremonial Coach or the Great Fire of London Experience. *Address:* 150 London Wall, EC2 (0171-600-3699). *Hours:* Tues-Sun 4:30pm-6:00pm. **U:** Barbican, St. Paul's, Moorgate. **B:** 141, 4, 502. **H C**

Guildhall
Built in 1411, restored in 1666 after the Great Fire and again in the late 1940's after WWII bomb damage, London's Guildhall has been the seat of civic government, the center for traditional ceremonies, and the setting for many famous trials. The Great Hall, where many of the Lord Mayor's ceremonies are still held, contains banners of the ancient Guilds, coats-of-arms, statues of British heroes, and replicas of the original wooden figures of Gog and Magog, mythical founders of pre-Roman London. *Address:* off Gresham St., EC2 (0171-606-3030). *Hours:* daily 10:00am-5:00pm. **U:** Bank, St. Paul's. **T**

Funny Papers
The National Museum of Cartoon Art is the UK's first museum devoted exclusively to the comics and cartooning. Despite its

unlikely setting in a staid office building, the museum is jam-packed with fabulous examples of the art form, from Hogarth lampoons to displays on the popular *Spitting Image* television show. *Address:* 15 St. Cross St. , EC1 (0171-404-4717) *Hours:* Mon-Fri, noon-6pm. **U:** St. Paul's. **C**

Telecom Technology Showcase
The Telecom Showcase explores the past, present, and future of Britain's telecommunications industry and demonstrates communications progress with hands-on activities, interactive videos, films, satellite hook-ups, and memorabilia. *Address:* 135 Queen Victoria St., EC4 (0171-248-7444). *Hours:* Mon-Fri 10:00am-5:00pm. **U:** St. Paul's, Blackfriars. **C**

The Temple
This tranquil warren of alleys, courtyards, gardens, and historic buildings derives its name from the Knights Templar, an ancient military order based there from the 12th-14th centuries. After dissolution of the Order, the area became the domain of the legal profession. It remains so today, with law office chambers and lecture and dining halls forming the Inns of Court in the Inner and Middle Temples. The Elizabethan hall of the Middle Temple is open to the public. Completed in 1574, the grand hall features ancient oak timbers, paneling, and rich carvings, along with portraits of British monarchs, stained glass, an incredible double hammer beam roof, and a table fashioned from timbers of Sir Francis Drake's *Golden Hind. Address:* Fleet St., EC4 (0171-353-4355). *Hours:* Mon-Fri 10:00am-noon & 3:00pm-4:00pm. **U:** Temple, Blackfriars. **B:** 6, 9, 11, 15. **T**

Temple Church
Erected by the Knights Templar in the late 12th century, the fetching Temple Church is modeled on the Church of the Holy Sepulcher in Jerusalem. Inside, there are fine stone effigies, 17th-century oak reredos designed by Wren, and an unusual penitent's cell from the 13th century. *Address:* King's Bench Walk, Inner Temple, EC4 (0171-353-1736). *Hours:* Mon-Sat 10:00am-4:00pm, Sun 1:00pm-4:00pm. **U:** Temple, Blackfriars. **B:** 6, 9, 11, 15. **H**

Old Bailey

True-life courtroom dramas unfold at London's Central Criminal Court, better known as the Old Bailey, where you're welcome to observe the progress of justice from the Public Galleries. Built on the site of the infamous Newgate Prison and execution yard, the Old Bailey is today the trial locale for many of Britain's most notorious criminal cases. The imposing gilded statue on the dome is "Lady Justice," with balancing scales in one hand and the sword of retribution in the other. *Address:* Newgate St., EC4 (0171-248-3277). *Hours:* Mon-Fri 10:30am-4:00pm. **U:** St. Paul's. **B:** 4, 6, 8, 9, 11, 15, 18, 22, 23, 502.

National Postal Museum

London's National Postal Museum contains the world's most comprehensive assemblage of postage stamps. The collection includes nearly every stamp issued since 1878, plus the archives of the Thomas de la Rue Co., which furnished stamps to 150 nations for a century. Although stamps are the centerpiece of the collections, the museum has other postal paraphernalia and special exhibitions. *Address:* King Edward St., EC1 (0171-239-5420). *Hours:* Mon-Fri 9:30am-4:30pm. **U:** St. Paul's. **B:** 4, 8, 22, 25. **T**

Clockmakers Company Collection

The Worshipful Company of Clockmakers collection was originally formed in the 18th century to provide instruction to apprentices. Along with exhibits illustrating the development of watches and clocks from the 1300's to the present, you'll find marvelous grandfather clocks, royal timepieces, Rococo confections, and specialized scientific instruments. *Address:* Guildhall, King St., EC2 (0171-606-3030). *Hours:* Mon-Fri 9:30am-5:00pm. **U:** Bank, Moorgate, Mansion House. **B:** 6, 8, 9, 11, 22, 502.

Stock Exchange

The London Stock Exchange, the world's second-largest, is the hub of British commercial finance. Visitors can view the modern trading floor from the public gallery, where guides and data banks explain the transactions. An explanatory film also runs eight times daily. *Address:* Old Broad St., EC2 (0171-588-2355). *Hours:* Mon-Fri 9:30am-3:30pm. **U:** Bank. **B:** 6, 8, 9, 15, 22, 25, 502.

Head Doorman Peter Costen outside the Lloyd's of London building. (photo: Janet Gill)

Leadenhall Market

Built in 1881 on the site of the original Roman Forum, this characteristic Victorian enclosed market derives its name from a lead-roofed medieval palace that once stood there. The impressive iron and glass arcades provide a wonderful setting for a bustling Cockney market. *Address:* Whittington Ave., EC3. *Hours:* Mon-Fri 7:00am-3:30pm. **U:** Bank, Monument. **B:** 6, 8, 9, 22. **C**

Prince Henry's Room

Prince Henry's Room is in one of the rare buildings to survive both the Great Fire of 1666 and the WWII Blitz. Built in the early 1600's, the house later became a tavern and was long thought to be a residence for Prince Henry, the eldest son of James I. Rich in Tudor and Jacobean decoration, the room now houses an exhibit of items relating to the diarist Samuel Pepys. *Address:* 17 Fleet St., EC4 (0171-353-7323). *Hours:* Mon-Sat 1:30pm-5:00pm. **U:** Blackfriars, Temple. **B:** 4, 6, 9, 11, 15, 23, 502.

Lloyd's of London

After 300 years, the world's leading insurer has opened its doors to the general public. The company's new $250 million City headquarters, designed by Richard Rogers, has become the most controversial building in London. Exterior glass elevators whisk visitors to the viewing gallery for superb London vistas and a unique perspective on the underwriting floor below. An exhibition explains the international insurance trade, and guides are available to interpret the mysteries of the underwriting business. *Address:* 1 Lime St., EC3 (0171-623-7100). *Hours:* Mon-Fri 10:00am-2:30pm. **U:** Bank, Monument. **T H** (call first)

St. Bride's Church and Crypt Museum

Meticulously restored in 1956 according to Sir Christopher Wren's original drawings and plans, St. Bride's is the eighth church Built on this site since the 6th century. The lovely wedding-cake spire rises 226 feet above the heart of the city. Deep inside, the Crypt Museum presents a capsule history of London and displays remnants of every building that has stood on the site, including Roman walls and floors. *Address:* Fleet St., EC4 (0171-353-1301). *Hours:* daily 8:30am-5:15pm. **U:** Blackfriars. **B:** 4, 6, 9, 11, 15, 23, 168

St. Bride's Printing Museum

St. Bride's Institute maintains an interesting collection of historic printing presses and related artifacts, as well as an extensive library on all types of printing techniques and materials. *Address:* Bride Lane, EC4 (0171-335-4660). *Hours:* Mon-Fri 9:30am-5:30pm. **U:** Blackfriars. **B:** 4, 6, 9, 11, 15, 23, 168.

Bank of England

"The Old Lady of Threadneedle Street" is the traditional center of London's financial community. Its well-designed museum explores three centuries of banking history and provides displays on the intricacies of contemporary finance and transactions. The museum also incorporates features of Sir John Soane's 18th-century bank building. *Address:* Threadneedle St., EC2 (0171-601-4444). *Hours:* Mon-Fri 10:00am-5:00pm. **U:** Bank. **B:** 6, 8, 9, 11, 15, 23, 502. **T H** (call first)

All Hallows by the Tower

Lovingly restored following WWII damage, All Hallows is the fourth church erected on this site adjacent to the Tower of London since the 7th century. The atmospheric Undercroft Museum has a terrific model of Roman Londinium, Roman mosaics and pottery, Saxon artifacts, and medieval memorials. Americans will be interested in church connections with William Penn and John Quincy Adams. *Address:* Byward St., EC3 (0171-481-2928). *Hours:* Mon-Fri 9:00am-5:30pm, Sat 10:30am-5:30pm. **U:** Tower Hill. **B:** 23, 42, 78. **T**

Royal Exchange

Officially opened in 1568 by Queen Elizabeth I, the present Royal Exchange is a splendid neo-classical edifice dating from the mid-19th century. Along with architectural considerations, the building is worth a visit to see the London International Financial Futures Exchange in action. Visitors to the Viewing Gallery can observe the colorful haggling of traders and learn about world financial markets from interactive videos. *Address:* Threadneedle & Cornhill Sts., EC3 (0171-623-0444). *Hours:* 11:30am-2:00pm. **U:** Bank. **B:** 6, 8, 9, 15, 22, 502.

Oldest Synagogue

The Spanish and Portuguese Synagogue, built by Iberian Jewish refugees in 1701, is Great Britain's oldest extant synagogue. Its welcoming interior is handsomely decorated with fine wood-work and seven brass chandeliers from the Netherlands. *Address:* Heneage Lane (off Bevis Marks), EC3 (0171-289-2573). *Hours:* call to arrange a tour. **U:** Liverpool St., Aldgate. **T**

College of Arms
Recently restored, the 17th-century College of Arms is the head-quarters of British heraldry. It continues to grant coats of arms to the worthy wealthy and houses official records of English and Welsh genealogy. If you're interested in tracing your family's roots, write well in advance to the Officer in Waiting. *Address:* Queen Victoria St., EC4 (0171-248-2762). *Hours:* Mon-Fri 10:00am-4:00pm. **U:** Blackfriars, St. Paul's. **B:** 4, 6, 9, 11, 15, 22, 23, 502.

Mansion House
This striking Palladian building, designed by George Dance in 1739, is the official residence of the Lord Mayors of London during their term in office. The hour-long tour includes the dramatic Egyptian Hall, decorated with 23-carat gold, and the opulent State Drawing Rooms. Impressive trappings of office, such as the Great Mace, Sword of State, Chain of Office, and 16th-century Pearl Sword presented by Queen Elizabeth I, are on display. *Address:* Walbrook St., EC4 (0171-626-2500, ext. 324). *Hours:* Tues-Thurs 11:00am-2:00pm, by appointment only. **U:** Bank, Mansion House. **B:** 6, 8, 9, 11, 15, 22, 502. **T**

St. Mary-Le-Bow
This famous Wren-designed church, with its spectacular white steeple, has a special place in the hearts of Londoners. Beginning in 1334, the Great Bell of Bow rang the curfew at night and provided a wake-up call every morning at 5:45. This practice continued until 1874, giving rise to the adage that "a real London Cockney must be born within the sound of Bow Bells." During WWII, St. Mary's chime was used as a BBC recognition signal and came to symbolize resistance to tyranny for people around the world. Beneath the church, a Norman crypt incorporates the walls of an earlier Saxon church. The Ecclesiastical Court of the Archbishop of Canterbury has met here since the 12th century. *Address:* Cheapside, EC2 (0171-248-5139). *Hours:* Mon-Fri 8:45am-4:00pm. **U:** St. Paul's, Bank, Mansion House. **B:** 8, 22, 25. **T**

The Lakeside Terrace at Barbican Centre.

Barbican Centre

This ultra-modern cultural arts complex, the largest of its kind in Europe, presents free concerts, exhibitions, plays, lectures, shows, and much more every day of the year. The classical and jazz concerts held in the Level Five foyer weekdays (noon-2:00pm and 5:00pm-7:30pm) are well worth a visit. The vast concrete complex also has cafes, bars, a restaurant, and shops. Guided tours leave at 12:15pm and 5:15pm. *Address:* Silk St., EC2 (0171-638-4141; 24-hour information: 0171-628-2295). *Hours:* Mon-Sat 9:00am-11:00pm, Sun noon-11:00pm. **U:** Barbican, Moorgate, St. Paul's, Liverpool St. **B:** 4, 9, 11, 21, 43, 76, 141, 502. **H T C**

City Livery Company Halls & Collections

Established in medieval times, London City Guilds (or Livery Companies) are the forerunners of contemporary British trade unions. Of the 96 Livery Companies in existence today, 30 retain Halls where their treasures are displayed. To visit these historic collections (some date to the early 12th century), you must obtain passes from the City of London Information Centre, St. Paul's Churchyard, EC4 (0171-606-3030).

Apothecaries
This Guild Hall, built in 1632, is the oldest standing and least altered Company quarters. It's notable for original oak woodworking, antique pharmacy jars and accoutrement, royal portraits, and medieval banners. *Address:* Blackfriars Lane, EC4.

Goldsmiths
As you might expect, the Worshipful Company of Goldsmiths possesses a spectacular collection of precious metal artifacts. One of the most intriguing pieces is a silver-gilt and crystal goblet used by Elizabeth I at her Coronation Banquet in 1558. *Address:* Foster Lane, EC2.

Fishmongers
This neo-classical Company Hall is in an imposing position overlooking the Thames. Rooms embellished with elaborate gold leaf decoration house medieval tapestries, precious metal plate, and royal portraits. *Address:* London Bridge, EC4.

Vintners
Built in 1671 and restored in 1948, this majestic Company Hall presents a fine collection, including a 15th-century tapestry of St. Martin of Tours and a 16th-century silver-gilt vessel in the shape of a milkmaid. *Address:* Upper Thames Street, EC4.

Armorers and Brasiers
Impressive weapons and armor, including suits worn by Elizabeth I's courtiers, are on display in this 19th-century Hall. *Address:* 81 Coleman St., EC2.

Ironmongers
Overshadowed by the neighboring Museum of London, this Company Hall appears to be from Tudor times, but actually dates from 1924. Its collection includes medieval funeral palls and 15th- through 20th-century plate. *Address:* Aldergate St., EC2.

St. Lawrence Jewry
The Corporation of London's official church is another Wren-designed revival. Modern restoration has reproduced the marvelous 17th-century gilded plasterwork and decoration. The best time to visit is 1:00pm on Monday or Tuesday for free, hour-long organ recitals. *Address:* Gresham St., EC2 (0171-600-9478).

Hours: Mon-Fri 8:00am-6:00pm, Sat 8:30am-5:00pm. **U:** Bank, St. Paul's, Moorgate. **B:** 8, 9, 11, 22, 23, 502.

Corporation of London Art Collection

When the Guildhall Art Collection opened to the public in 1886, the Corporation of London had been accumulating works of art for more than two centuries. Today, the collection includes hundreds of portraits of British royalty, military heroes, and London dignitaries, as well as strong collections of 18th- and 19th-century paintings and sculpture. Special exhibitions run throughout the year. *Address:* Gresham St., EC2 (0171-606-3030, ext. 2856). *Hours:* Mon-Fri 10:00am-5:00pm. **U:** Bank, Moorgate, St. Paul's. **B:** 6, 8, 9, 11, 15, 22, 23, 502.

Guildhall Library Collection

Founded in 1420, the Guildhall Library contains a peerless collection of manuscripts, maps, books, and illustrations on the history of the City of London. The Corporation of London's extensive collection of watercolors, prints, and drawings is on display in the Library Print Room. *Address:* Guildhall West Wing, Gresham St., EC2 (0171-606-3030). *Hours:* Mon-Sat 9:30am-5:00pm. **U:** Bank, Moorgate, St. Paul's. **B:** 6, 8, 9, 11, 15, 22, 23, 502. **T**

Court of Common Council

The City of London Borough Council meetings, still held at the Guildhall, are open to the general public. Proceedings traditionally begin with an entertaining ceremony involving the Lord Mayor, the official Swordbearer, the Macebearer, and the City Marshal. *Address:* Guildhall (call 0171-606-3030 to verify dates). *Hours:* Thursday 1:00pm-3:00pm.

St. Mary Abchurch

Miniature in scale, St. Mary Abchurch is yet another of Wren's wonderful churches arising from urban revival after the Great Fire. Inside, hidden completely from exterior view, there's a fabulous painted dome, as well as magnificent original decoration by Grinling Gibbons. *Address:* Abchurch Lane (off Cannon St.), EC4 (0171-626-0306). *Hours:* Mon-Fri 10:00am-4:00pm. **U:** Cannon St., Monument. **B:** 6, 8, 9, 11, 15, 22, 23.

Chartered Insurance Institute Museum

This unusual museum contains artifacts and documents relating to the history of insurance companies and fire-fighting. Antique firemen's gear and equipment, along with models, illustrations, and firemark plates, are on display. *Address:* 20 Aldermanbury, EC2 (0171-606-3835). *Hours:* Mon-Fri 9:30am-5:00pm. **U:** Moorgate. **B:** 4, 141, 501.

Broadgate Centre

This contemporary entertainment and commercial complex, with shops, bars, restaurants, and exhibit spaces, surrounds a spectacular glassed-in arena. On weekdays (April-Nov) there are free concerts, shows, and dance performances at noon. *Address:* Eldon St., EC2 (0171-588-6565). *Hours:* daily, 24 hours. **U:** Liverpool St. **H C**

St. Giles Cripplegate

Overshadowed by the behemoth Barbican Centre, St. Giles dates to 1090, when a Norman church was first built on this site. The current building is a post-WWII restoration. Rich in history (John Milton is buried in the chancel, Martin Frobisher in the south aisle, and Oliver Cromwell married there in 1620), St. Giles provides an atmospheric backdrop for free lunchtime concerts. *Address:* Fore St., EC2 (0171-606-3630). *Hours:* Mon-Fri 9:30am-2:00pm, Sun 8:00am-4:00pm. **U:** Barbican, Moorgate. **B:** 8, 22, 25. **H**

Guildhall School of Music and Drama

Free concerts, plays, recitals, and other performance events are presented frequently at this Barbican Centre venue. Call for a free program of events and tickets. *Address:* Silk St., EC2 (0171-628-2571). **U:** Barbican, Moorgate. **B:** 4, 9, 11, 21, 141. **H C**

Daily Express Building

In dramatic contrast to the City's many historic sites, the Daily Express Building is a dazzling piece of Art Deco design. Built in 1931, it's enveloped in a chromium and black glass curtain wall. The highly stylized interior is highlighted by generous use of black and variegated marble, metals, and ebony. *Address:* 121 Fleet St., EC4. *Hours:* Mon-Fri 8:00am-5:00pm. **U:** Black-friars. **B:** 4, 6, 9, 11.

Sir John Soane's Museum

The volume and variety of items displayed in this unique gem of a museum are best described as staggering. In 1833, architect John Soane secured an Act of Parliament guaranteeing the perpetuation of his private museum on the condition that nothing be changed or removed. His accumulated treasure contains Babylonian, Egyptian, Greek, Persian, and Roman antiquities; paintings, engravings, and sketches by the likes of Turner, Canaletto, Hogarth, Piranesi, and Watteau; and thousands of sculptures, vases, and assorted bric-a-brac from around the world. The best way to see the collection is by taking the lecture tour on Saturday at 2:30pm. *Address:* 13 Lincoln's Inn Fields, WC2 (0171-4052107). *Hours:* Tues-Sat 10:00am-5:00pm. **U:** Holborn. **B:** 5, 68, 77A, 170, 188. **T C**

The Inns of Court

These tranquil enclaves epitomize the traditional London that most visitors come to experience. Dating to the 13th century, each Inn (or Honorable Society of Barristers) is designed along a collegiate plan much like Oxford and Cambridge, with its own chambers, chapels, common rooms, and gardens. All London barristers must join an Inn before they can be called to the Bar.

Lincoln's Inn

Dickensian in atmosphere, Lincoln's is probably the most picturesque and unaltered Inn. Entry from Chancery Lane is through the original gatehouse built in 1518. Once through the archway, the buildings are mainly Tudor restorations in brick. *Address:* Chancery Lane, WC2 (0171-405-1393). *Hours:* Mon-Fri, dawn-dusk.

Gray's Inn

Founded in the 14th century, Gray's today presents a 16th-century face. Much restoration was necessary following extensive WWII bomb damage. Sir Francis Bacon, the Inn's most illustrious member, designed the lovely gardens. *Address:* 22 High Holborn, WC1 (0171-405-8164). *Hours:* Mon-Fri 9:30am-5:00pm.

Staple Inn

The heart of this small complex is an incredible row of original, 16th-century, half-timbered buildings, which provide a rare glimpse of pre-Great Fire London. *Address:* High Holborn, WC1. *Hours:* Mon-Fri 9:00am-5:00pm.

St. Etheldreda's

One of the finest examples of Gothic architecture in Great Britain and the only pre-Reformation Catholic Church in London, St. Etheldreda's was Built in 1291 by the Bishop of Ely as a chapel for his episcopal house. The vicissitudes of time and war have left little of the original church except the walls, with impossibly delicate tracery, and the spooky crypt, with its eight-foot thick masonry walls and medieval roof timbers. Statues on the walls and contemporary stained glass windows commemorate Catholic martyrs of Tudor religious persecution. *Address:* Ely Place, EC1 (0171-405-1061). *Hours:* daily 7:30am-5:30pm. **U:** Chancery Lane, Farringdon. **B:** 4, 6, 9, 11, 15.

Marx Memorial Library

When Soviet President Mikhail Gorbachev visited London in 1984, his first stop was the Marx Memorial Library. Opened in 1933 to mark the 50th anniversary of Karl Marx's demise, the library today houses an exceptional collection of social, political, and philosophic literature, as well as an unparalleled collection of Socialist and labor movement memorabilia. The Lenin Room, where the Bolshevik avatar edited the party paper *Iskra*, is also open to view. *Address:* 37a Clerkenwell Green, EC1 (0171-253-1485). *Hours:* Mon & Fri 2:00pm-6:00pm, Tues-Thurs 2:00pm-9:00pm, Sat 11:00am-1:00pm. **U:** Farringdon. **B:** 19, 38, 55, 503.

Museum of the Order of St. John

Situated in an early 16th-century gatehouse that was once the entrance to the medieval priory of the Knights of St. John of Jerusalem, this museum presents an interesting collection of weapons, armor, medals, ceramics, illuminated manuscripts, paintings, and furniture. The same building houses the St. John Ambulance Museum, which explores the history of the Ambulance Brigade. *Address:* St. John's Lane, EC1 (0171-253-6644). *Hours:* Tues-Sat 10:00am-4:00pm. **U:** Farringdon, Barbican. **T**

Mount Pleasant Post Office

Handling nearly three million letters and parcels daily, this is the largest mail sorting office in the world. The two-hour guided tour explores the complex and offers views of the unique Post Railway. Operating 70 feet below ground, the automated railway transports mail to seven stations between Paddington and Whitechapel. *Address:* Farringdon Rd., EC1 (0171-239-2191). Tours: Mon-Thurs 10:30am, 2:30pm, and 7:30pm. **U:** Farringdon. **T**

Royal Courts of Justice
With its many towers, pilasters, pillars, and vaulted Great Hall, the neo-Gothic courthouse is a splendid example of exuberant Victorian architecture. Visitors are welcome in the public galleries of the 60 courtrooms. There's also a museum of legal gear, costumes, and documents. *Address:* Strand, WC2 (0171-936-6470). *Hours:* Mon-Fri 9:00am-4:00pm. **U:** Temple, Chancery Lane, Aldwych. **B:** 6, 9, 11, 15. **H**

Museum of the United Grand Lodge of England
The mystery and mysticism of Freemasonry are revealed for the uninitiated on the free tour of their Art Deco Grand Temple. The vast collection of Masonic jewels, medals, regalia, and precious metal works is the world's most extensive. Even if you find the rituals and handshakes a bit silly, the majestic Grand Temple is well worth a visit. *Address:* Great Queen St., WC2 (0171-831-9811). *Hours:* Mon-Fri 10:00am-5:00pm. **U:** Holborn, Covent Garden. T **H**

Hunterian Museum
This bizarre museum evolved from the private anatomical collection of the 18th-century surgeon and researcher John Hunter. Along with stuffed animals, fossils, and the results of anatomical experiments, displays include skeletons of dwarfs, giants, and infamous London murderers. Definitely not for the squeamish! *Address:* Lincoln's Inn Fields, WC2 (0171-405-3474). *Hours:* Mon-Fri 10:00am-5:00pm, by appointment only. **U:** Holborn, Aldwych.

London Lesbian and Gay Centre
Britain's largest lesbian and gay social center and meeting place has a disco, bars, restaurant, theater, workshops, and meeting spaces. *Address:* 67 Cowcross St., EC1 (0171-608-1471). *Hours:* Mon-Thurs 5:30pm-11:00pm, Fri-Sat noon-1:00am, Sun 1:00pm-6:00pm. **U:** Farringdon. **B:** 4, 8, 141.

St. Bartholomew-the-Great

Founded in 1123 by a courtier of Henry I, the castellated and turreted "St. Bart's" of today is only a shadow of the great Augustinian priory that once stood there. After Henry VIII dissolved the priory in 1539, the great church fell into disarray for 350 years and was used as a stable, factory, and printers' workshop. A century of restoration has revealed a 13th-century gateway and the sublime 14th-century Lady Chapel. Free lunchtime concerts are a regular feature. *Address:* West Smithfield, EC1 (0171-606-5171). *Hours:* daily, 8:00am-4:30pm. **U:** Barbican, St. Paul's, Farringdon. **B:** 9, 11, 43, 76, 141. **H T**

Covent Garden
and Trafalgar Square

Covent Garden Market

Once a bustling "fruit 'n veg" market, Covent Garden has become a trendy shopping, meeting, and entertainment venue. The renovated, glass-canopied arcades are now occupied by pubs, bookstores, wine bars, and cafes, as well as stalls and pushcarts selling crafts, jewelry, antiques, and clothing. The Covent Garden Piazza provides a great backdrop for ongoing street theater, and magicians, jugglers, musicians, clowns, and acrobats perform daily. *Address:* King St., WC2 (0171-836-9136). *Shop Hours:* Mon-Sat 9:30am-9:00pm. **U:** Covent Garden, Leicester Square, Charing Cross. **B:** 1, 3, 6, 13, 15, 68, 77A, 159. **H C**

Jubilee Market

This large indoor market retains some of the flavor of the original Covent Garden. Though you won't find many bargains these days, you will find crafts, collectibles, toys, records, novelties, gifts, and clothes. *Address:* Henrietta St., WC2 (0171-836-2139). *Hours:* Mon-Fri 7:00am-5:00pm, Sat-Sun 9:00am-5:00pm. **U:** Covent Garden, Leicester Square, Charing Cross. **B:** 1, 3, 6, 15, 68, 77A, 159. **C**

Ecology Centre

The West End's "Green" hub presents changing exhibits on international ecological issues, provides information on the Green movement in Europe, sells environmentally conscious products, and offers health food at reasonable prices. *Address:*

45 Shelton St., WC2 (0171-379-4324). *Hours:* Mon-Sat 10:00am-9:00pm. **U:** Covent Garden, Leicester Square.

Africa Centre

Britain's best resource for information on African culture, travel, and politics also houses an art gallery, crafts shop, lecture hall, and restaurant. *Address:* 38 King St., WC2 (0171-836-1973). *Hours:* daily, 10:00am-6:30pm. **U:** Covent Garden, Leicester Square.

St. Paul's Covent Garden

With its splendid portico overlooking Covent Garden Piazza, this Inigo Jones-designed 17th-century church is rich in theatrical associations. In 1662, the first ever "Punch & Judy" show in Britain played there; the opening scenes of *Pygmalion* and *My Fair Lady* were set there; and actress Vivien Leigh is buried there. *Address:* King St., WC2 (0171-836-5221). *Hours:* Mon-Fri 9:00am-4:30pm. **U:** Covent Garden, Leicester Square.

Photographers' Gallery

Both rising stars and longtime masters of photography display at this exciting gallery and exhibition center. *Address:* 5 & 8 Great Newport St., WC2 (0171-831-1772). *Hours:* Tues-Sat 11:00am-7:00pm. **U:** Leicester Square, Covent Garden. **B:** 14, 19, 29, 38. **H**

Glass House

Visitors are always welcome to observe London's foremost glass blowers at work in this combined gallery and workshop. *Address:* 65 Long Acre, WC2 (0171-836-9785). *Hours:* Mon-Fri 10:00am-6:00pm, Sat 11:00am-4:30pm. **U:** Covent Garden.

London Silver Vaults

Silver lovers won't want to miss this underground complex of vaults and strongrooms with a lustrous array of historic and contemporary cutlery, hollow ware, plate, and objets d'art. *Address:* 53 Chancery Lane, WC2 (0171-242-3844). *Hours:* Mon-Fri 9:00am-5:00pm, Sat 9:00am-12:30pm. **U:** Chancery Lane. **B:** 6, 9, 11, 15. **H T**

Royal Society of Arts

Housed in an impressive 18th-century neo-classical building designed by Robert Adam, the Society presents lectures on art,

Covent Garden & Trafalgar Square

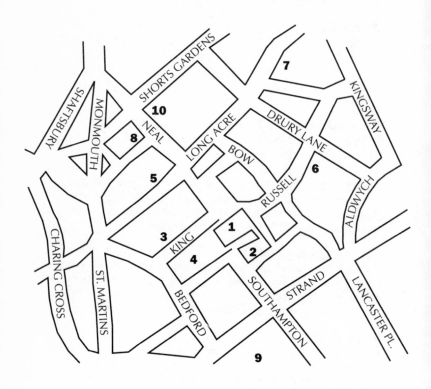

1. Covent Garden
2. Jubilee Market
3. Africa Centre
4. St. Paul's
5. Glass House
6. Theatre Royal
7. Freemasons Hall
8. Contemporary Arts
9. Royal Society of Arts
10. London Ecology Centre

science, technology, communication, commerce, and architecture. The highlight of the lavishly decorated building is the Great Room, with James Barry's series of paintings *The Progress of Human Knowledge*. Admission to the free lecture program is by ticket, obtainable by calling the Secretary of the Society. *Address:* 8 John Adam St., WC2 (0171-930-5115). **U:** Charing Cross. **B:** 1, 3, 12, 15B, 53, 88. **T**

Cleopatra's Needle
This 3,500-year old granite obelisk was presented to the British in 1819 by the Ottoman Viceroy of Egypt. When it was finally erected in 1878, a time capsule with various items of Victoriana was buried underneath. *Address:* Victoria Embankment, WC2.

Contemporary Applied Arts
Special exhibits of works in ceramic, metal, sculpture, glass, fiber, and other media are the bill of fare at this Covent Garden gallery. *Address:* 43 Earlham St., WC2 (0171-836-6993). *Hours:* Mon-Sat 10:00am-5:00pm. **U:** Leicester Square, Covent Garden. **B:** 14, 19, 22B, 29, 38.

Drury Lane Theatre Royal
Built in 1812, the present Drury Lane is the fourth theater built on this site—and London's loveliest. Rich in decor and tradition, the interior has a domed entrance, ornate rotunda, and a sumptuous Grand Salon. *Address:* Drury Lane, WC2 (0171-836-8108). *Hours:* tours by appointment only. **U:** Covent Garden. **T**

St. Mary-Le-Strand
This diminutive Baroque jewel of a church was built by James Gibbs in 1717. Known affectionately as "the cabby's church," it's elegantly decorated with superb plasterwork and stained glass. *Address:* Strand, WC2. *Hours:* Mon-Fri 8:30am-5:00pm. **U:** Aldwych, Temple.

National Gallery
Great Britain's leading collection of European paintings incorporates all major schools of art from the 13th through 20th centuries. The diverse collection includes works by Titian, Raphael, Rembrandt, Rubens, Van Eyck, Velazquez, Van Gogh, Cezanne, Gainsborough, Matisse, and scores of other masters.

Unique among Europe's premier museums in its policy of exhibiting its entire collection, the National Gallery's sheer size and the wealth of the collection makes a viewing strategy essential. *Address:* Trafalgar Square, WC2 (0171-839-3321). *Hours:* Mon-Sat 10:00am-6:00pm, Sun 2:00pm-6:00pm. **U:** Leicester Square, Charing Cross. **B:** 1, 3, 6, 9, 11, 12, 13, 15, 24, 29, 53, 88. **H T**

National Portrait Gallery

Founded in 1856 "to acquire portraits of men distinguished in the history of this country," the National Portrait Gallery's first acquisition was a painting of William Shakespeare. Today, the Italianate gallery, opened in 1896, houses a permanent collection of 10,000 paintings, sculptures, drawings, photos, and videos of famous men and women in British history from the age of the Tudors to the present. Contemporary additions include portraits of Mick Jagger, Princess Diana, and Andy Warhol. *Address:* 2 St. Martin's Place, WC2 (0171-930-1552). *Hours:* Mon-Fri 10:00am-5:00pm, Sat 10:00am-6:00pm, Sun 2:00pm-6:00pm. **U:** Charing Cross. **B:** 1, 3, 6, 9, 11, 12, 13, 15, 23, 53, 77, 88, 170. **T**

Nelson's Column

Perhaps London's most famous landmark, this 185-foot monument, erected in 1843, commemorates Admiral Horatio Nelson's defeat of Napoleon at the Battle of Trafalgar in 1805. The fluted granite column is surmounted by a 16-ton stone statue of Nelson. Four grand bronze lions stand sentinel at the base and make a great playground for children and the frequent demonstrators in Trafalgar Square. *Address:* Trafalgar Square, WC2. **U:** Charing Cross. **B:** 3, 6, 9, 11, 12, 13, 15, 29, 77, 159.

St. Martin-in-the-Fields

Set amidst the bustle of Trafalgar Square, James Gibbs' majestic church is an island of tranquility and beauty. Completed in 1726, St. Martin is universally recognized by its soaring steeple and striking Corinthian portico. Inside, the dusky interior is decorated with understated elegance: the dark woodwork is by Grinling Gibbons, the windows are Venetian glass, and the ceiling is in white and gold Italian fretting. St. Martin's long association with orchestral music makes it a superb venue for lunchtime concerts

Nelson's Column. (BTA photo)

on Mondays and Tuesdays. *Address:* Trafalgar Square, WC2 (0171-930-1862). *Hours:* daily, 7:30am-7:30pm. **U:** Charing Cross. **B:** 3, 6, 9, 11, 12, 13, 15, 29, 77, 159. **H**

Bloomsbury

British Library

The Exhibition Galleries of the British Library, housed in the East Wing of the British Museum, display just a fraction of the world's richest collection of books and related materials. In the Grenville Library, you'll find English, Byzantine, and Carolingian illuminated manuscripts. The Manuscript Salon has two of the four copies of the *Magna Charta*, the *Lindisfarne Gospels* of 698, and the 4th-century *Codex Sinaiticus*, one of the earliest manuscripts of the Bible. The King's Library, built in 1823 to house the library of George III, displays fabulous illuminated scrolls and manuscripts in Coptic, Hebrew, Persian, Arabic, Armenian, Chinese, and Japanese, as well as specimens of early printed books and items relating to Shakespeare. Treasures of the Map Library include thousands of maps, charts, and town plans of colonial North America. Best known of the Library's halls is the Round Reading Room with its immense, cast-iron dome and 25 miles of shelving. Tours available from 11:00am-4:00pm. *Address:* Great Russell St., WC1 (0171-636-1544). *Hours:* Mon-Sat 10:00am-5:00pm, Sun 2:30pm-6:00pm. **U:** Tottenham Court, Goodge St., Russell Square, Holborn. **T**

Coram's Fields City Farm

This idyllic pastoral retreat in the heart of Bloomsbury comes complete with goats, sheep, ducks, rabbits, an aviary, and all the aromas of the English countryside. *Address:* 93 Guilford St., WC1 (0171-837-6138). *Hours:* April-Oct: daily 8:30am-9:00pm; Nov-March: Mon-Fri 8:30am-4:30pm. **U:** Russell Square, Holborn. **B:** 10, 14, 19, 77A. **C**

The Building Centre

This exhibition and information complex provides a showcase for London's booming building industry. You'll find special shows by architects, interior designers, developers, restorers, and builders. *Address:* 26 Store St., WC1 (0171-637-1022).

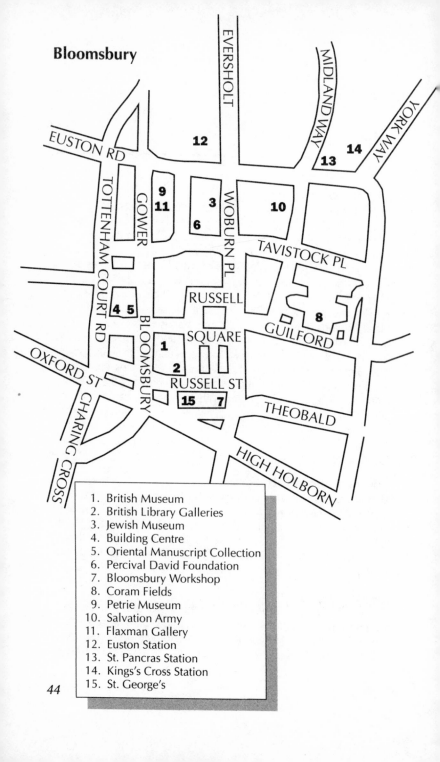

Bloomsbury

1. British Museum
2. British Library Galleries
3. Jewish Museum
4. Building Centre
5. Oriental Manuscript Collection
6. Percival David Foundation
7. Bloomsbury Workshop
8. Coram Fields
9. Petrie Museum
10. Salvation Army
11. Flaxman Gallery
12. Euston Station
13. St. Pancras Station
14. Kings's Cross Station
15. St. George's

Hours: Mon-Fri 9:30am-5:00pm, Sat 10:00am-3:00pm. **U:** Goodge St., Tottenham Court. **B:** 10, 14, 19, 24, 73. **H T**

Oriental Manuscript and Book Collection

With over 600,000 books, manuscripts, and artifacts covering the cultures of Asia, the Middle East, and North Africa, this is one of the world's foremost classical Oriental archives. The collection includes the earliest printed book, medieval Japanese woodcut prints, and priceless Chinese oracle bones dating from 2000 BC. *Address:* 14 Store St., WC1 (0171-636-1544). *Hours:* Mon-Fri 9:30am-5:00pm, Sat 9:30am-1:00pm. **U:** Goodge St., Tottenham Court. **B:** 10, 14, 19, 24, 73. **T**

Percival David Foundation of Chinese Art

This extraordinary collection of vases, plates, pots, and amphorae, donated to London University by its namesake, provides a ceramic history of Chinese design from the 8th through 18th centuries. Many pieces were once owned by Chinese Emperors and bear the imperial insignia. *Address:* 53 Gordon Square, WC1 (0171-387-3909). *Hours:* Mon-Fri 10:30am-5:00pm. **U:** Goodge St., Russell Square, Euston Square. **B:** 8, 10, 14, 19, 30, 188. **T**

Bloomsbury Workshop

Literati shouldn't miss this quirky gallery/bookshop, which displays and sells works by and about the Bloomsbury Group. Along with first editions, memoirs, biographies, and memorabilia, you'll find paintings, sketches, sculpture, and prints. *Address:* 12 Galen Place, WC1 (0171-405-0632). *Hours:* Mon-Fri 10:00am-6:00pm. **U:** Holborn, Russell Square. **B:** 8, 19, 22, 38, 55. **H**

Petrie Museum of Egyptian Archaeology

Sir Flinders Petrie, a pioneer of modern archaeology and Egyptology, assembled this detailed collection of Egyptian antiquities. Displays include the oldest known linen garment in the world, tomb stelae, faience statuary, jewelry, hieroglyphics, and funerary relics. *Address:* University College London, Gower St., WC1 (0171-387-7050). *Hours:* Mon-Fri 10:00am-5:00pm. **U:** Euston Square. **B:** 10, 14, 30, 68, 73, 77A. **T**

British Museum

Four and a half million visitors a year ramble through Britain's grandest museum to gaze at the world's greatest assemblage of

The British Museum. (BTA photo)

international antiquities. Housed in an immense neo-classical edifice, this collection of treasures from the dawn of civilization to the present is so vast you'd need weeks to see everything. Highlights among the nearly boundless trove include the Head of Sophocles, the Rosetta Stone, the Nereid Monument, the Sutton Hoo Treasure, the Portland Vase, and the finest concentration of Egyptian sculpture, jewelry, paintings, and sarcophagi outside Egypt. Go on weekdays to avoid the crowds. *Address:* Great Russell St., WC1 (0171-636-1555). *Hours:* Mon-Sat 10:00am-5:00pm, Sun 2:30pm-6:00pm. (Open until 9:00pm the first Tuesday each month.) **U:** Tottenham Court, Goodge St., Russell Square, Holborn. **B:** 7, 8, 14, 19, 38, 68, 73, 77, 144. **T C H** (call first)

Salvation Army Museum

Located on the second floor of the Salvation Army Publishing Building, the museum recounts the story of this unique religious movement. Among the displays are memorabilia, photos, documents, and possessions of the founder of the Army, General William Booth, and his followers. The exhibition provides a glimpse of daily life in the 19th century and the dedication required to challenge poverty. *Address:* 117 Judd St., WC1 (0171-387-1656). *Hours:* Mon-Fri 9:30am-3:30pm. **U:** King's Cross. **T**

Flaxman Gallery

Set under the impressive central dome of University College, the Gallery contains works of the noted British sculptor John Flaxman. Celebrated in the early 19th century as a neo-classical designer, Flaxman's monuments and statues adorn public spaces and churches throughout the country. *Address:* Gower St., WC1 (0171-387-7050). *Hours:* Mon-Fri 10:00am-5:00pm. **U:** Warren St., Euston, Euston Square. **B:** 10, 14, 30, 73, 135.

St. George's Bloomsbury

Designed by Nicholas Hawksmoor, Britain's greatest Georgian church builder, St. George's has a splendid Corinthian portico, an obelisk-shaped spire, and a fine neo-classical interior. It's worth a visit for the richly gilded plasterwork by master plasterer Isaac Mansfield. *Address:* Bloomsbury Way, WC1 (0171-405-3044). *Hours:* Mon-Fri 10:00am-3:00pm. **U:** Tottenham Court Rd., Holborn. **B:** 8, 19, 22B, 38, 55.

Museum of the Institute of Ophthalmology

This unique collection of the University of London consists primarily of specialized scientific instruments. Early microscopes designed by Culpeper and van Leeuwenhoek in the 17th century are displayed, along with a variety of historic and unusual eyeglasses from around the world. *Address:* Judd St., WC1 (0171-387-9621). *Hours:* Mon-Fri 9:30am-5:00pm. **U:** King's Cross.

The Henry VII Chapel at Westminster Abbey. (BTA photo)

Westminster and St. James's

Westminster Abbey

Westminster Abbey remains the preeminent example of the glory of medieval English architecture. From its 6th-century inception as East Saxon King Sebert's church, Westminster Abbey has been associated with the British Crown. The first Abbey was built by Edward the Confessor, who died and was buried there within a week of the official dedication on December 28, 1065. In the early 13th century, King Henry III began revamping the Abbey in the style of French Gothic cathedrals. Later additions, including towers by Wren and Hawksmoor in the 18th century, have kept to the soaring Gothic spirit of flying buttresses, gabled transepts, and tracery windows. All English monarchs since William the Conqueror in 1066 have been crowned there, and many are interred within the Abbey's walls. Hundreds of famous Britons, especially literary figures like Chaucer, Dickens, and Lewis Carroll, are also memorialized in Westminster. *Address:* Broad Sanctuary, SW1 (0171-222-5152). *Hours:* Mon-Sat 8:00am-6:00pm (free admission to nave and cloisters). On Wednesday from 6:00pm-8:00pm, the entire Abbey is free and photography is permitted. **U:** St. James's Park, Westminster. **B:** 3, 11, 12, 24, 29, 53, 70, 76, 77, 88, 109, 155, 159, 172, 184. **H T**

Westminster College Garden

The 900-year old College Garden, reputed to be the oldest in the United Kingdom, is a little-known gem at the heart of the Westminster Abbey complex. The herb and flower gardens are replicas of those kept by Benedictine monks in the Middle Ages. There are wonderful concerts in the College Garden on Thursdays at noon in August and September. *Hours:* April-Sept: Thurs 10:00am-6:00pm; Oct-March: 10:00am-4:00pm

Westminster Hall

Built in 1097 for William Rufus, son of William the Conqueror, Westminster Hall is the only surviving part of the original Palace

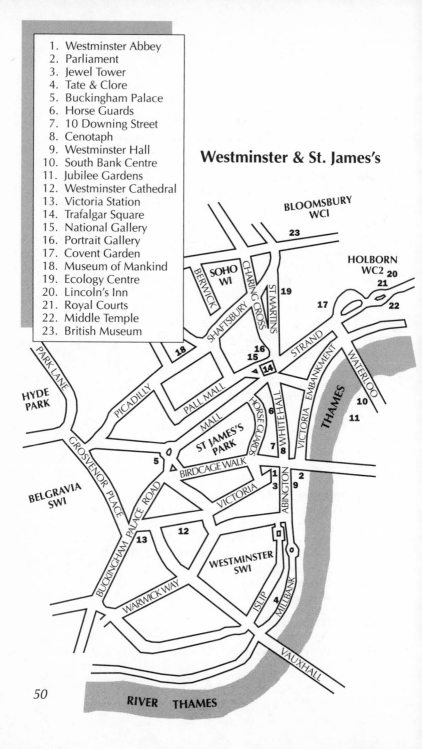

1. Westminster Abbey
2. Parliament
3. Jewel Tower
4. Tate & Clore
5. Buckingham Palace
6. Horse Guards
7. 10 Downing Street
8. Cenotaph
9. Westminster Hall
10. South Bank Centre
11. Jubilee Gardens
12. Westminster Cathedral
13. Victoria Station
14. Trafalgar Square
15. National Gallery
16. Portrait Gallery
17. Covent Garden
18. Museum of Mankind
19. Ecology Centre
20. Lincoln's Inn
21. Royal Courts
22. Middle Temple
23. British Museum

Westminster & St. James's

of Westminster. The hall was the scene of royal feasts, ceremonies, jousting, and historic trials until the 18th century. The superb, 14th-century hammer beam roof is probably the finest in Great Britain. *Address:* Parliament Square, SW1 (0171-219-3000 or 0171-219-4273). *Hours:* Tours by appointment only. Call for details. **U:** Westminster. **B:** 3, 11, 12, 24, 29, 39, 53, 70, 76, 77, 88, 109, 155, 170, 172, 184. **T**

St. Margaret's Westminster

Standing in the shadow of the great Abbey, the ancient St. Margaret's is often overlooked by London visitors. Built in the mid-11th century by Edward the Confessor, the church was substantially altered in the late 15th century and again in the 19th. John Milton, Samuel Pepys, and Winston Churchill married at St. Margaret's, and Walter Raleigh was buried there in 1618 after his execution at the Palace Yard across the road. The interior is rich in memorials and has some of London's loveliest stained glass. *Address:* Parliament Square, SW1 (0171-222-6382). *Hours:* daily, 9:30am-5:30pm. **U:** Westminster, St. James's Park. **B:** 3, 11, 12, 24, 29, 39, 53, 70. **H**

Houses of Parliament

The immense, neo-Gothic Houses of Parliament stand on the site of the ancient Palace of Westminster, which burned to the ground on October 16, 1834. Covering eight acres, with 1,000 rooms and two miles of corridors, the bicameral legislative palace was designed by Charles Barry and Augustus Pugin and built between 1840 and 1860. The magnificent House of Lords is lavishly decorated in gilt and scarlet, with red, buttoned leather benches and the golden Throne of the Sovereign. The House of Commons, originally completed in 1852, was destroyed in a 1941 bombing raid and rebuilt simply, in late-Gothic style. Admission is free to both Strangers' Galleries, but seats are limited and difficult to get. Americans may be able to get tickets from the U.S. Embassy (24 Grosvenor Square, W1, phone 0171-499-9000). The best bet is to join the queue at St. Stephen's entrance Monday through Thursday after 2:00pm or Friday before 9:00am. Tours of Parliament run weekdays from 10:00am-4:30pm, but, again, you must get tickets far in advance from the Embassy or from a Member of Parliament. *Address:* Parliament Square, SW1 (0171-219-4272 or 0171-219-3000).

Hours: Mon-Thurs 2:30pm-10:00pm, Fri 9:45am-3:00pm. **U:** Westminster. **B:** 3, 11, 12, 24, 29, 39, 53, 70, 76, 77, 88, 109, 155, 159, 170, 172, 184. **H T**

Victoria Tower Gardens

This lovely riverside garden is best known for the Burghers of Calais, a superb bronze group by Rodin, and the statue of suffragette Emmeline Parkhurst. The quiet park is a welcome refuge from the tourist bustle and a great spot for an alfresco lunch. *Address:* Abington St., SW1. *Hours:* daily, 7:00am-dusk. **H**

Clore Gallery

The recently opened Clore Gallery, adjacent to the Tate, is home to a true national treasure, the J.M. Turner Collection. The ethereal works of the greatest English painter are now hung in James Stirling's controversial, post-Modern gallery. *Address:* Millbank, SW1 (0171-821-7128). *Hours:* Mon-Sat 10:00am-5:50pm, Sun 2:00pm-5:50pm. **H T**

The Changing of the Guard

Get in position early to see London's most famous ceremony! The Changing of the Queen's Guard occurs in the Buckingham Palace forecourt daily from April to mid-August and on alternate days the rest of the year. The best locations for viewing the ceremony are from the gates of the palace, but you can see the colorful troops in their scarlet and blue uniforms all along the parade route. *Address:* Buckingham Palace, Queens Gardens, SW1 (0171-730-3488). *Hours:* daily, 11:30am. **U:** St. James's Park, Green Park, Victoria. **B:** 2, 2B, 11, 14, 16, 19, 22, 24, 25, 29, 30, 36, 36B, 38, 39, 52, 55, 70, 73, 74, 137, 149, 185, 500, 507. **C**

Tate Gallery

The Tate Gallery opened in 1897 with a mandate to show "modern" British art—"modern" being defined as post-1790. Today, the Tate has a dual role as a national gallery of British painting and a museum of 20th-century art. The Tate's British collection boasts works by Hogarth, Gainsborough, Reynolds, Constable, Millais, and William Blake. The museum has an outstanding collection of Cubist works, Impressionists and Post-Impressionists, Surrealists, and American Abstract Expressionists. Art lovers throng the Tate on weekends, so plan to visit during the week if possible. *Address:* Millbank, SW1 (0171-821-

Arrive early for a good view of the Changing of the Guard at Buckingham Palace. (BTA photo)

1313). *Hours:* Mon-Sat 10:00am-6:00pm, Sun 2:00pm-6:00pm.
U: Pimlico. **B:** 2, 3, 36, 77A, 88, 185, 507. **H T**

St. James's Park

London's oldest royal park was acquired in 1532 by Henry VIII, but the contemporary, picturesque park was completely re-designed by John Nash in the 1820's. St. James's has fine prom-enades, a romantic, Chinese-style lake, a bird sanctuary, and sweeping vistas of palaces, the spires of Whitehall, and Westmin-ster Abbey. The park is a great place for a picnic, an afternoon stroll, or a glimpse of the Queen's Guard. *Address:* The Mall, SW1 (0171-930-1793). *Hours:* daily, dawn-dusk. **U:** St. James's Park, Westminster. **B:** 2, 2B, 3, 11, 12, 14, 19, 24, 25, 29, 36, 52, 53, 55, 70, 73, 74, 77, 88, 137, 149, 159, 170, 185. **H C**

Berkshire and Westminster Dragoons Museum

Exhibits illustrate the histories of the Dragoons, the Territorial Army, the Royal Armored Corps, the Imperial Yeomanry, and the old Volunteer Militia of Westminster. *Address:* 1 Elverton St., SW1 (0171-865-7995). *Hours:* Mon-Fri 9:00am-5:00pm. **U:** St. James's Park. **B:** 2B, 11, 16, 24, 25, 29, 36, 38, 52.

Westminster Cathedral

Relatively few tourists take the time to visit this magnificent, Byzan-tine-style cathedral. Designed by John Benchly in 1895, Westmin-ster Cathedral is the British headquarters of the Roman Catholic Church and a symphony in brick, marble, and stone. The vast inte-rior, 360 feet long with the widest nave in England, is richly deco-rated with mosaics made of hundreds of kinds of marble and lit by thousands of small candles. Don't miss the alabaster,15th-century statue of the Virgin and Child in the south transept. *Address:* Ashley Place, SW1 (0171-834-7452). *Hours:* daily, 7:00am-8:00pm. **U:** Victoria. **B:** 10,11,24,29, 70, 76,149, 507. **T**

National Portrait Gallery Archive

Housed in outstanding Nash terraces overlooking St. James's Park, the Archive contains Britain's most extensive collection of portrait engravings and a massive library of historic volumes on heraldry, costume, art history, lithographs, and caricatures. *Ad-dress:* 15 Carlton House Terrace, SW1 (0171-930-1552). *Hours:* Mon-Fri 9:30am-5:00pm. **U:** Charing Cross. **B:** 3, 11, 12, 24, 29, 53, 77, 88, 159, 172.

Changing of the Guard at Horse Guards

Less crowded than the Buckingham Palace ceremony, the Changing of the Guard at the headquarters of the Commander of the Home Forces is nonetheless colorful and exciting. The mounted Queen's Life Guards, in scarlet tunics with white plumed helmets, ride from their Hyde Park barracks via the Mall to the courtyard of the Horse Guards for the 25-minute ceremony. *Address:* Whitehall, SW1. *Hours:* Mon-Sat 11:00am, Sun 10:00am. **U:** Charing Cross, Embankment. **B:** 3, 11,12, 24, 29, 53, 77, 88, 172. **H C**

London Buddhist Society

The London Buddhist Society promotes a better understanding of the three main schools of Buddhism: Tibetan, Zen, and Theravada. There are free lectures, classes, seminars, and art exhibits daily. *Address:* 58 Eccleston Square, SW1 (0171-834-5858). *Hours:* Mon-Fri 2:00pm-6:00pm, Sat 2:00pm-5:00pm. **U:** Victoria. **B:** 11, 16, 24.

Henry VIII's Wine Cellar

Deep below the Ministry of Defense, King Henry VIII's wine cellar is one of the few intact remnants of the Whitehall Palace, destroyed by fire in 1698. The eerie cellar is a vaulted undercroft with ten crypt-like bays. *Address:* Horse Guards Ave., SW1 (0171-921-4849). *Hours:* Sat 2:00pm-5:00pm, by appointment only. **U:** Charing Cross, Westminster. **B:** 3, 12, 29, 53, 77A, 88. **T**

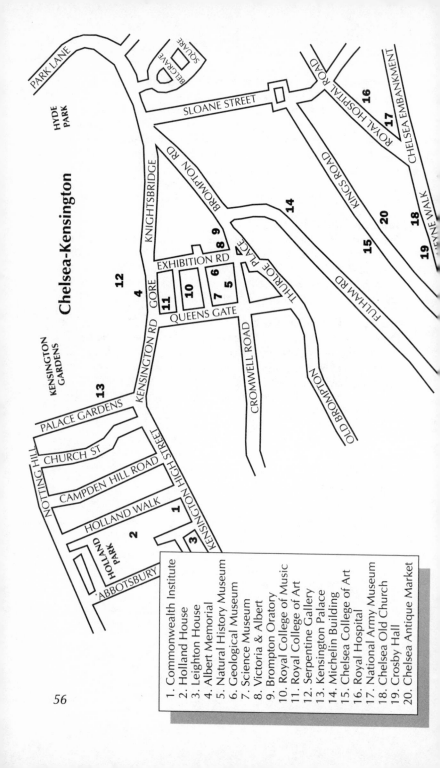

Chelsea-Kensington

1. Commonwealth Institute
2. Holland House
3. Leighton House
4. Albert Memorial
5. Natural History Museum
6. Geological Museum
7. Science Museum
8. Victoria & Albert
9. Brompton Oratory
10. Royal College of Music
11. Royal College of Art
12. Serpentine Gallery
13. Kensington Palace
14. Michelin Building
15. Chelsea College of Art
16. Royal Hospital
17. National Army Museum
18. Chelsea Old Church
19. Crosby Hall
20. Chelsea Antique Market

Chelsea, Knightsbridge, and South Kensington

Crosby Hall

Built between 1466-1475, this great medieval hall originally stood in Bishopsgate and was part of the residence of wool mechant Sir John Crosby. William Shakespeare, Sir Thomas More, and King Richard III all stayed at Crosby Hall. The finely paneled hall, with its rare painted hammer beam roof and three-tier oriel window, was moved to Chelsea in 1910 to rescue it from demolition. *Address:* Cheyne Walk, SW3 (0171-352-9663). *Hours:* daily, 10:00am-noon & 2:00pm-4:00pm. **U:** Sloane Square. **B:** 137.

Chelsea Old Church

The original church predates the Norman invasion but has been much altered by restoration and WWII bombing. In the 1950's, the entire church was reconstructed—from the Saxon foundations up—so it now looks substantially as it did in 1528 when Sir Thomas More added a private chapel. Look for superb monuments—a l l rescued from the rubble—to Lady Jane Cheyne, Sarah Colville, and Sir Thomas Lawrence. *Address:* Cheyne Walk, SW3 (0171-352-5627). *Hours:* daily, 10:00am-6:30pm. **U:** Sloane Square. **B:** 19, 45, 49, 137, 219.

Royal Hospital Chelsea

Founded in 1682 by King Charles II as a home for old soldiers, the Royal Hospital continues to serve that function today, providing a retreat for some 400 "Chelsea Pensioners." The stately, Wren-designed buildings are beautifully set in a Thames-side park. Visitors are welcome to view the Great Hall and Chapel, both providing excellent examples of 17th-century decoration, design, and furnishing. There's also an interesting museum with Wellington memorabilia, objects relating to the Royal Hospital, and a fine collection of militaria. *Address:* Royal Hospital Rd., SW3 (0171-730-0161). *Hours:* Mon-Sat 10:00am-noon & 2:00pm-4:00pm. (From April-Sept, open Sundays 2:00pm-4:00pm.) **U:** Sloane Square. **B:** 11, 19, 22, 137. **T**

National Army Museum

The National Army Museum tells the rousing story of the British and Commonwealth soldier through five centuries of war and peace. Exhibits in the permanent galleries include weapons, uniforms, medals, paintings, sculpture, silver, and ceramics. Videos, reconstructions, and models detail the soldier's story from Tudor times to the present. Among the museum's most important displays are Wellington's telescope from the Battle of Waterloo, the order that launched the Charge of the Light Brigade, the skeleton of Napoleon's favorite horse, and paintings by Gainsborough. *Address:* Royal Hospital Rd., SW3 (0171-730-0717). *Hours:* daily, 10:00am-5:30pm. **U:** Sloane Square. **B:** 11, 19, 22, 39, 137. **H T**

IBA Broadcasting Gallery

The informative and entertaining Independent Broadcasting Authority Gallery presents the story of radio and television broadcasting. Exhibits range from the earliest motion pictures through contemporary satellite technology. There's a replica of the first TV studio at Alexandra Palace, an in-depth exploration on how the news is covered, a modern TV studio, multi-media shows, and exhibits on the future of broadcasting. *Address:* 70 Brompton Rd., SW3 (0171-584-7011). *Hours:* Tours Mon-Fri at 10:00am, 11:00am, 2:00pm, 3:00pm. **U:** Knightsbridge. **B:** 14, 30, 74, C1. **T H**

Chelsea Antique Market

London's oldest indoor antique market is also one of the best places to find bargains on antiquarian books, antique jewelry, period clothing, theatrical souvenirs, scientific instruments, and art nouveau objects. *Address:* 245 King's Rd., SW3 (0171-352-5689). *Hours:* Mon-Sat 10:00am-6:00pm. **U:** Sloane Square. **B:** 11, 19, 22.

Brompton Oratory

Built in 1884, the Brompton Oratory of St. Philip Neri is an ornate, Italian Baroque-style Catholic church. The wide and lofty nave of the Oratory is festooned with classical statues of the saints — including some from the ancient Cathedral of Sienna in Italy — and richly decorated in colorful marbles. The Oratory is famous for its choral and music recitals and has an enormous 4,000-pipe organ. *Address:* Brompton Rd., SW3 (0171-589-4811). *Hours:* daily, 6:30am-8:00pm. **U:** South Kensington. **B:** 14, 30, 74.

Michelin Building
The recently restored Michelin Building is London's most extravagant example of art nouveau architecture. Designed originally as an advertisement for the French tire manufacturer, the building is flamboyantly decorated with tiles, mosaics, stained glass, and glass cupolas. This temple of kitsch now houses a restaurant, a bar, the Conran Shop, and a publishing company. *Address:* Fulham Rd., SW3 (0171-581-9393). *Hours:* Mon-Sat 9:30am-6:00pm. **U:** South Kensington. **B:** 14, 30, 45, 49, 74, 503, C1. **H C**

Chelsea College of Art and Design
Frequently changing exhibitions of painting, sculpture, interior design, ceramics, and graphics are held at the Chelsea College of Art. Henry Moore's sculpture *Two-Piece Reclining Figure* decorates the forecourt. *Address:* Manresa Rd., SW3 (0171-351-3844). *Hours:* Mon-Sat 8:30am-5:00pm. **U:** Sloane Square, South Kensington. **B:** 11, 19, 22. **H**

Antiquarius
With over 150 stalls, Chelsea's most popular indoor antiques market offers a tremendous diversity in relics, bygones, and bric-a-brac. Among the specialties, you'll find antiquarian books, objet d'art, Victorian jewelry, glassware, and engravings. *Address:* 135 King's Rd., SW3 (0171-351-5353). *Hours:* Mon-Sat 10:00am-6:00pm. **U:** Sloane Square. **B:** 11, 19, 22.

Italian Cultural Institute
The Italian Cultural Institute presents exhibitions of Italian art, hosts literary events, and promotes Italian culture. *Address:* 39 Belgrave Square, SW1 (0171-235-1461). *Hours:* Mon-Sat 9:30am-5:00pm. **U:** Knightsbridge. **B:** 9, 14, 30.

Spanish Institute

Created to promote Spanish culture and language, the Institute exhibits Spanish artists and photographers, shows films, and sponsors lectures on contemporary literature and social issues. *Address:* 102 Eaton Square, SW1 (0171-235-1484). *Hours:* Mon-Thurs 10:00am-6:00pm. **U:** Victoria.

Victoria and Albert Museum

Known affectionately as "Britain's attic," the Victoria and Albert is the world's greatest decorative arts museum. Within ten acres of gallery space there's an eclectic treasure trove that encompasses Medieval, Gothic, Renaissance, Byzantine, Islamic, and Asian art, carpets, musical instruments, four centuries of European fashion, pieces from the Russian Crown Jewels, stained glass, enamels, ceramics and porcelain, armor and weapons, and much, much more. Try to join one of the daily gallery talks at 2:15pm. Note: a voluntary admission contribution is requested, but not required. *Address:* Cromwell Rd., SW7 (0171-938-8500 or 938-8349). *Hours:* Mon noon-5:50pm, Tues-Sat 10:00am-5:50pm, Sun 2:30pm-5:50pm. **U:** South Kensington. **B:** 14, 3Q 45, 49, 74, 503, C1. **H T C**

Science Museum

A must for kids of all ages, the Science Museum is a real hands-on attraction with working models, interactive exhibits, and innumerable buttons to push and handles to pull. Permanent displays explore the history of science and technology—from waterwheels to interstellar travel. Popular exhibits include the earliest surviving locomotives, WWII aircraft, the Space Gallery (with a real lunar command module), and the "Food for Thought" Gallery. *Address:* Exhibition Rd., SW7 (0171-938-8111 or -8123). *Hours:* daily, 4:00pm-6:00pm. **U:** South Kensington. **B:** 9, 14, 30, 45, 49, 73, 74. **H T C**

Natural History Museum

Alfred Waterhouse's extraordinary, neo-Romanesque colossus makes a perfect setting for the world's greatest collection of animals, plants, fossils, and minerals. The striking, cathedral-like, turn-of-the-century museum is focused on the coming century with new galleries on ecology, the environment, and wildlife. The Dinosaur Gallery, with reconstructed behemoths, and the

"Creepy-Crawly" Gallery are always big hits with the kids. *Address:* Cromwell Rd., SW7 (0171-938-9123). *Hours:* free Mon-Fri 4:00pm-6:00pm, Sat & Sun 5:00pm-6:00pm. **U:** South Kensington. **B:** 14, 30, 45, 49, 74, 264, C1. **H T C**

Geological Museum

Founded in 1835 to display collections of the British Geological Survey, this ever-popular museum presents self-contained, thematic exhibitions on earth sciences. Don't miss the much acclaimed "Story of the Earth," which tells the five-billion-year history of our planet, the unparalleled Gemstone Collection, "Britain before Man," and the stirring "Earthquake Room," which convincingly simulates the real thing. *Address:* Exhibition Rd., SW7 (0171-938-8765). *Hours:* free Mon-Fri 4:00pm-6:00pm, Sat & Sun 5:00pm-6:00pm. **U:** South Kensington. **B:** 9, 14, 30, 45, 49, 52, 73, 74. **H T C**

National Sound Archive

This branch of the British Library preserves millions of recordings from the 1890's to the 1990's, plus over 90,000 musical scores. The collection incorporates folk and ethnic music from around the world, classical and popular music, and dramatic recordings from the Royal Shakespeare Company, the National Theatre, and British stage companies. The Archive's collection also includes recording devices ranging from primitive wax cylinders to compact discs. A free listening service is open to the public. *Address:* 29 Exhibition Rd., SW7 (0171-589-6603). *Hours:* Mon-Fri 10:00am-5:30pm. **U:** South Kensington. **B:** 9, 14, 30, 52, 73, 74. **T**

Royal Geographic Society

Housed in the gabled, brick Lowther Lodge, the Royal Geographic Society is dedicated to world exploration and geographical education. Eminent past members include explorers Stanley, Livingstone, and Robert Falcon Scott. The Society's collection of 750,000 maps and atlases is surpassed only by the Library of Congress and the British Library. Along with rare historic maps, you'll find memorabilia of great explorers, a fine collection of paintings, and 125 years of travel photos. *Address:* Kensington Gore, SW7 (0171-589-5466). *Hours:* Mon-Fri 10:00am-5:00pm. **U:** South Kensington. **B:** 9, 33, 49, 52, 73.

Albert Memorial

The Albert Memorial is the epitome of Victorian style, taste, and mawkish melodrama. Sir George Gilbert Scott designed the ostentatious, neo-Gothic folly in 1872 as a tribute to the Prince Consort from his grieving people. The intricate, 175-foot memorial surmounts four flights of granite steps and is crowned by a "wedding cake" canopy replete with pinnacles, mosaics, and gewgaws. A much romanticized, 14-foot bronze statue of Albert sits at the center, surrounded by allegorical statues and friezes. At the base of the pedestal, monumental carved mammals represent the Continents. This is one memorial not to be missed! *Address:* Kensington Gardens, SW7. *Hours:* open 24 hours. **U:** South Kensington, Kensington High Street, Knightsbridge, Gloucester Road. **B:** 9, 33, 45, 49, 52, 73.

Royal College of Music Portraits Department

The Royal College of Music presents an engaging collection of portraits, statues, engravings, prints, and photographs of famous musicians, as well as historic mementos from the music world. The College of Music is housed in a noteworthy, late-Victorian building in dark red brick and gray stone, with decorated step gables and pepperpot turrets. *Address:* Prince Consort Rd., SW7 (0171-589-3643). *Hours:* Mon-Fri 10:00am-5:30pm. **U:** South Kensington, Gloucester Road. **B:** 9, 33, 49, 52, 73. **T**

Goethe Institute

Organized to promote German culture, the Goethe Institute hosts frequently changing exhibitions by German artists and photographers, lectures, readings, and classic and contemporary German films. *Address:* 50 Prince's Gate, SW7 (0171-581-3344). *Hours:* Mon-Thurs 10:00am-8:00pm, Sat 10:00am-6:00pm. **U:** South Kensington. **B:** 9, 33, 49, 52, 73.

Royal College of Art

The Henry Moore Gallery of the Royal College of Art presents exceptional shows by Britain's new artists. Recent exhibits have included painting, sculpture, traditional crafts, and printmaking. *Address:* Kensington Gore, SW7 (0171-584-5020). *Hours:* Mon-Fri 10:00am-6:00pm. **U:** Gloucester Road, South Kensington. **B:** 9, 33, 49, 73. **H**

National Art Library

The National Art Library is a branch of the Victoria and Albert Museum, but actually predates the museum by 20 years. The Library's peerless collection of over one million volumes contains some of the most beautiful books, manuscripts, and illustrations ever produced. Highlights include medieval Bibles and manuscripts illustrated by post-Impressionist painters. The Library holds regular exhibits from the magnificent collection. *Address:* Cromwell Rd., SW7 (0171-589-6371, ext. 331). *Hours:* Mon-Thurs & Sat 10:00am-5:00pm.**U:** South Kensington. **B:** 14, 30, 45, 49, 74, 503, C1. **H T**

Baden-Powell House

Any Scout worth his merit badges will want to visit this museum and memorial to Lord Baden-Powell, the "Founder of Scouting." The exhibition traces his achievements and exploits with memorabilia, mementos, and photos. *Address:* Queen's Gate, SW7 (0171-584-7030). *Hours:* daily, 9:00am-6:00pm. **U:** Gloucester Road, South Kensington. **B:** 14, 30, 45, 49, 74, 264, C1. **H C T**

Kensington Gardens

This 275-acre royal park serves as the "backyard" to Prince Charles's Kensington Palace, but don't count on a glimpse of any Royals. You will, however, find Queen Anne's Orangery, the peaceful Sunken Garden, Italian fountains, the Round Pond (always crowded with model sailboats), the Serpentine Gallery, fabulous Barbara Hepworth sculptures, and puppet shows on Monday in the summer at 11:00am and 3:00pm. *Address:* Kensington Rd., W8 (0171-724-2826). *Hours:* daily, 5:00am-dusk. **U:** Queen's Way, Lancaster Gate, High Street Kensington, Knightsbridge. **H C**

Serpentine Gallery

The Arts Council of Great Britain presents an innovative series of contemporary art shows at this charming gallery overlooking Kensington Gardens. *Address:* Kensington Gardens, W2 (0171-402-6075). *Hours:* April-Sept: daily 10:00am-7:00pm; Oct-March: 10:00am-4:00pm. **U:** Knightsbridge, Lancaster Gate, Kensington High St. **B:** 9, 52, 73. **H**

Hyde Park

A place for strolling, band concerts, royal salutes, and parades, Hyde Park is a vast green space in the heart of central London. Speaker's Corner, across from the triumphal Marble Arch in the northeast corner of Hyde Park, has been a celebrated forum for free speech since 1872. On Sunday, soapbox philosophers, politicians, rabble-rousers, and demagogues of every bent provide continuous entertainment. *Address:* bound by Bayswater Rd., Park Lane, Carriage Rd., and Kensington Palace Gardens. *Hours:* daily, dawn-midnight. **U:** Marble Arch, Lancaster Gate, Hyde Park Corner, Knightsbridge, Queensway, Kensington High St. **B:** 2A, 6, 7, 8, 10, 12, 16, 30, 36, 74, 82, 88, 135, 503. **H C**

Spy vs. Spy

London's Sikorski Museum, named after the general who was commander of the Free Polish forces in World War II, has unique exhibits on wartime history, the Enigma code machine, and spycraft. *Address:* 20 Prince's Gate, SW7 (0171-589-9249). *Hours:* Mon-Fri 2:00pm-4:00pm; Sat 10:00am-5:00pm.

Boutique Brews

Established in 1995, Freedom Brewing Company is on the crest of Britain's new wave in microbrewing. Freedom's brewmaster has offered *London for Free* readers an open invitation to visit the facility and sample his beer fresh from the lagering tanks. The company's principal beverage, Freedom Pilsner Lager, is crafted to the exacting standards of the German purity law of 1516, which limits the ingredients of beer to water, hops, malt, and yeast. *Address:* Parson's Green, Fulham, SW6 (0171-731-7372). *Hours:* daily by appointment. **U:** Parson's Green. **B:** 28, 44, 220.

Kensington

Commonwealth Institute

Unmistakable with its hyperbolic paraboloid copper roof, the Commonwealth Institute is an exciting center for the promotion of the countries of the British Commonwealth. The Institute's program of permanent and temporary exhibitions reflects the diversity of the Commonwealth peoples and cultures through multi-media shows, festivals, theater, musical performances, films, art and photo exhibits, workshops, and seminars. If you're planning a journey to a Commonwealth nation, be sure to visit the Institute's Information Centre while in London. The expert staff will provide all you need to know about the country and region. *Address:* Kensington High St., W8 (0171-603-4535). *Hours:* Mon-Sat 10:00am-5:00pm, Sun 2:00pm-5:00pm. **U:** Kensington High Street, Holland Park, Earl's Court. **B:** 9, 10, 27, 28, 31, 33, 49, 701. **H T C**

Leighton House

A simple brick exterior belies the exotic interior of Kensington's Leighton House. Built in 1866 by Lord Frederic Leighton, the great classical painter and president of the Royal Academy, the House's richly decorated rooms were early expressions of the English Aesthetic Movement. Its most memorable feature is the stunning Arab Hall, added in 1879 to display Leighton's collection of Islamic tiles. This remarkable domed structure has a fabulous stained glass cupola, a mosaic floor, Moorish fountain, and ornate tiles from Syria, Egypt, Iran, and Turkey. Leighton House also presents an excellent collection of High Victorian art, with important works by Millais, Burne-Jones, Crane, Caldicott, and Leighton himself. *Address:* 12 Holland Park Rd., W14 (0171-602-3316). *Hours:* Mon-Sat 11:00am-5:00pm. **U:** Kensington High Street, Holland Park. **B:** 9, 27, 28, 33, 49, 73. **T**

Holland House and Park

Set in a pastoral and secluded park, Holland House was built in 1606 for the courtier Sir Walter Cope. Seriously damaged by WWII bombing, only one wing (now the King George VI Youth Hostel), the Orangery, Ballroom, and Ice House remain. The delightful park has an 18th-century Dutch tulip garden, formal rose gardens, and a remarkable 30-acre woodland with exotic plants, woodpeckers, owls, peacocks, and small mammals. Daily summer events include puppet and magic shows, children's theater, concerts, and the ever-popular Inflatable Culture Cave. *Address:* Holland Walk, W8 (0171-603-6956). *Hours:* daily, 7:30am-10:00pm. **U:** Kensington High Street, Holland Park. **B:** 9, 10, 27, 28, 31, 33, 49. **H C**

The Orangery and Ice House

The early 17th-century Orangery and Ice House, surviving remnants of Holland House, are unique sites for changing exhibitions. Recent shows have featured Indian watercolors, Japanese stoneware, woodcarvings, undersea ceramics, batik, and traditional blacksmithing. *Address:* Holland Walk, W8 (0171-603-1123). *Hours:* daily, 11:00am-7:00pm. **U:** Holland Park, Kensington High Street. **B:** 9, 10, 27, 28, 31, 49.

Kensington Town Hall

The Royal Borough of Kensington and Chelsea Town Hall is the site of year-round events including antique shows, decorative arts exhibitions, fashion fairs, doll and toy shows, crafts exhibits, seminars, and conferences. *Address:* Hornton Street, W8 (0171-937-5464). *Hours:* daily, 9:00am-6:00pm. **U:** Kensington High Street. **B:** 9, 10, 27, 28, 31, 33, 49, 701, 704.

Portobello Road

This century-old tradition has become one of London's most famous flea markets and tourist attractions. The narrow road is crammed with shops and hundreds of stalls selling antiques, bric-a-brac, period clothing, books, food, jewelry, and trendy junk. It's liveliest on Saturdays, when there are street performers, buskers, and a cosmopolitan crowd. *Address:* Portobello Rd., W11. *Hours:* Mon-Fri 8:00am-3:00pm, Sat 8:00am-5:00pm. **U:** Notting Hill Gate, Ladbroke Grove. **B:** 12, 28, 31, 52.

Saatchi Collection

Begun in 1970 by Charles and Doris Saatchi, the collection is now housed in a magnificent converted warehouse. One of Britain's largest and finest private art collections, the Saatchi consists of nearly 700 paintings and sculptures by artists such as Andy Warhol, Frank Stella, David Hockney, and Robert Ryman. Exhibits from the collection change on a rotating basis every six months. *Address:* 98A Boundary Rd., NW8 (0171-624-8299). *Hours:* noon-6:00pm. **U:** St. John's Wood. **B:** 159.

Mayfair and Piccadilly

Museum of Mankind

Drawing on the British Museum's Department of Ethnography collection, the splendid (and often overlooked) Museum of Mankind presents exhibitions on the indigenous peoples of Asia, Africa, Oceania, and the Americas. The museum is renowned for its daring, intricate reconstructions, which in recent years have included an Amazon rainforest, a Yemeni *souk,* and an Indonesian village. There's also an ongoing display of treasures acquired by early European explorers and adventurers. *Address:* 6 Burlington Gardens, W1 (0171-437-2224). *Hours:* Mon-Sat 10:00am-5:00pm, Sun 2:30pm-6:00pm. **U:** Piccadilly, Green Park, Oxford Circus. **B:** 3, 6, 9, 12, 19, 38, 53, 88, 159. **H T C**

Burlington Arcade

Built in 1819, this famous covered promenade is a perfectly preserved slice of refined Regency London. The rarefied atmosphere is jealously guarded by uniformed beadles, who ensure no one whistles, sings, runs, or opens an umbrella in the arcade. *Address:* Piccadilly and Old Bond St., W1. *Hours:* Mon-Sat 10:00am-5:00pm. **U:** Piccadilly Circus, Green Park. **B:** 9, 14, 19, 22. **H**

St. James Piccadilly

Another gem by Christopher Wren, St. James makes a tranquil retreat amidst the hurly-burly of Piccadilly. The barrel vaulted interior is opulently decorated with plaster work and gilded wood carvings by Grinling Gibbons — an atmospheric venue for lunchtime recitals and concerts. On Friday and Saturday, there's an excellent crafts market in the courtyard. *Address:* 197 Piccadilly, W1 (0171-734-4511). *Hours:* daily 8:30am-6:30pm. **U:** Piccadilly Circus. **B:** 3, 6, 9, 12, 13, 14, 15, 22.

SOTHEBY'S LOT 128
£9,800,000
US DOLLAR 19,502,000
FR FRANC 96,040,000
DM MARK 28,616,000
SW FRANC 24,206,000
IT 1000's 21,609,000
JP 1000's 2,508,800

Bidding begins at Sotheby's for "The Lock" by Constable. The painting sold for a record $20 million. (Photo courtesy Sotheby's)

Sotheby's

The sales and exhibition halls of the world's largest and oldest antiques dealer are open to the general public. There are daily sales, with everything from Beatles memorabilia to Egyptian scarabs on the auction block. *Address:* 34 New Bond St., W1 (0171-493-8080). *Hours:* Mon-Fri 9:30am-4:30pm. **U:** Bond St., Green Park, Oxford Circus. **B:** 6, 7, 8, 10, 15, 16A, 137, 503.

Design Centre

The Design Centre displays outstanding examples of contemporary British craftsmanship. Frequently changing shows cover everything from toys to tableware. *Address:* 28 Haymarket, SW1 (0171-839-8000). *Hours:* Mon & Tues 10:00am-6:00pm, Wed-Sat 10:00am-8:00pm, Sun 1:00pm-6:00pm. **U:** Piccadilly Circus.

Wallace Collection

Lady Wallace bequeathed this remarkable collection of paintings, furniture, and applied arts to the nation in 1897. Included among the array of treasures are works by Hals, Rubens, Rembrandt, Van Dyck, Titian, and Gainsborough. Exquisite Limoges enamels, Sevres porcelains, oriental lacquer ware, Rococo chandeliers, and Venetian glass are just a few examples of the wealth of the applied arts collection. The Wallace rivals some of Europe's finest galleries—don't miss it! *Address:* Hertford House, Manchester Square, W1 (0171-935-0687). *Hours:* Mon-Sat 10:00am-5:00pm, Sun 2:00pm-5:00pm. **U:** Bond St., Marble Arch. **H T**

All Saints

Designed by William Butterfield in 1859, All Saints is a masterpiece of Gothic Revival architecture. The exterior makes original use of colored bricks for decorative effect, and the sumptuous interior is richly embellished with travertine, granite, marble, and alabaster. *Address:* 7 Margaret St., W1 (0171-636-1788). *Hours:* daily 7:00am-7:00pm. **U:** Oxford Circus. **B:** 7, 8, 10, 25, 73, 503.

Courtauld Institute of Art

Established in 1932 in a handsome Robert Adam mansion, the Courtauld Institute contains the most comprehensive archive of Western painting in the world. This unique collection of two million reproductions encompasses 900 years of art history. *Address:* 19 Portman Square, W1 (0171-935-9292). *Hours:* Mon-Fri 10:00am-6:00pm. **U:** Bond St., Marble Arch. **B:** 2B, 6, 8, 10, 13, 74, 159.

Free Haircuts

You can't beat the price at the London College of Fashion, where men can get a haircut at no charge by hair styling students. *Address:* 20 John Prince's St., W1 (0171-493-0790).

Hours: open Mon-Fri; call for class times. **U:** Oxford Circus. **B:** 7, 8, 10, 25, 73, 503.

British Architectural Drawings Collection

Housed in a splendid Robert Adam building, the Royal Institute of British Architects' collection incorporates designs by European and American architects, as well as numerous architectural models. The wide-ranging displays include Elizabethan designs and works by Le Corbusier, van der Rohe, Palladio, and Frank Lloyd Wright. The Institute's Heinz Gallery presents frequent exhibitions by contemporary British architects. *Address:* 21 Portman Square, W1 (0171-580-5533). *Hours:* Mon-Fri 10:00am-1:00pm. (Open Saturday during exhibitions.) **U:** Bond St., Marble Arch. **B:** 2B, 6, 8, 10.

Scottish Gallery

The London branch of the celebrated Edinburgh Scottish Gallery presents a variety of contemporary Scottish artists in its recently opened Mayfair location. *Address:* 28 Cork St., W1 (0171-287-2121). *Hours:* Mon-Fri 10:00am-6:00pm, Sat 10:00am-1:00pm. **U:** Piccadilly.

British Dental Association Museum

No doubt the best museum on dentistry in Europe, the exhibits are designed to illustrate the tremendous advances in the field over the centuries. The most interesting displays are reconstructions of two 19th-century dentist offices. *Address:* 64 Wimpole St., W1 (0171-935-0875). *Hours:* Mon-Fri 10:00am-4:00pm. **U:** Bond St.

Free Lunch

Forget that old adage about a free lunch and head for the Soho headquarters of the Hare Krishna Society, where members serve free, generous helpings of delicious vegetarian fare. *Address:* 9 Soho St., W1 (0171-437-3662). *Hours:* Mon-Sat 11:00am-6:00pm. **U:** Tottenham Court. **B:** 14, 19, 22, 24, 25, 29, 38.

Polish Cultural Institute

The Polish Institute provides a wide range of cultural activities, including concerts, lectures, films, videos, and artistic exhibitions. *Address:* 34 Portland Place, W1 (0171-636-6032). *Hours:* Mon-Fri 8:30am-5:00pm. **U:** Regents Park. **B:** 30, 135, C2.

Grays Antique Market

At Grays, over 200 stalls housed in two gigantic Victorian buildings deal in militaria, jewelry, bygones, toys, art nouveau objects, and leather goods. *Address:* 58 Davies St., W1 (0171-629-7034). *Hours:* Mon-Fri 10:00am-6:00pm. **U:** Bond St. **B:** 6, 7, 8, 12, 13, 16A.

British Music Information Centre

An unparalleled compilation of records, discs, taped music, scores, and music videos is maintained by this private organization. Free concerts, recitals, and shows run on Tuesday and Thursday at 7:30pm. *Address:* 10 Stratford Place, W1 (0171-499-8567). *Hours:* Mon-Fri 10:00am-5:00pm. **U:** Bond Street. **B:** 6, 7, 8,10.

Royal Arcade

Built in 1879, this stylish, ornate promenade has appealed to the upscale market since opening day. Royals from Queen Victoria to the Queen Mum have done their shopping there. *Address:* connects Old Bond St. with Albemarle St., W1. *Hours:* Mon-Sat 10:00am-5:00pm. **U:** Piccadilly. **B:** 9, 14, 19, 22, 25, 38.

Ben Uri Gallery

The Ben Uri Gallery displays works by Jewish artists from Great Britain and abroad, including many works by Marc Chagall. *Address:* 21 Dean St., W1 (0171-437-2852). *Hours:* Mon-Fri 10:00am-5:00pm. **U:** Tottenham Court. **B:** 7, 10, 14, 22B, 55, 73, 503.

House of St. Barnabas

A modest exterior belies extraordinary interior decoration in this surprising Soho landmark. Built in 1750 as a private home, the mansion later served as a shelter for homeless "gentlewomen." Exceptional design features include beautiful plasterwork ceilings and walls, an unconventional crinoline staircase, rococo chandeliers, and a diminutive, neo-Gothic chapel. *Address:* 1 Greek St., W1 (0171-437-1894). Tours: Wed 2:00pm-4:45pm, Thurs 10:45am-1:00pm. **U:** Tottenham Court. **B:** 7, 8, 10, 14A, 19, 22, 25, 55. **T**

Berwick Street Market

There's been a market here since 1810, selling a wide variety of products and produce. The stalls around Rupert Street are known especially for their bargains on clothes. *Address:* Soho. *Hours:* Mon-Sat 9:00am-5:00pm. **U:** Piccadilly, Oxford Circus, Leicester Square.

Liberty's

Liberty's is the quintessentially British department store. Founded in 1875 by Arthur Liberty and long associated with the Aesthetic Movement, the company specializes in elegant fabrics, fashion, and furniture. The 1922 Tudor building was constructed with teak and oak timbers salvaged from the Royal Navy's last two sailing ships. Inside, unique wooden galleries surround a central atrium. *Address:* Great Marlborough St. & Regent St., W1 (0171-734-1234). *Hours:* Mon-Wed & Fri-Sat 9:30am-6:00pm, Thurs 9:30am-7:30pm. **U:** Oxford Circus. **B:** 3, 6, 8, 12, 13, 16A, 137, C2.

National Monuments Record

Established in 1908 by Royal Warrant, the National Monuments Record surveys and records archaeological sites and historic buildings. The voluminous collection of drawings, photographs, and prints provides a nostalgic glimpse of bygone Britain. *Address:* 23 Savile Row, W1 (0171-734-6010). *Hours:* Mon-Fri 10:00am-5:30pm. **U:** Piccadilly Circus, Oxford Circus. **H**

London Diamond Centre

The in-depth tour of this glittering exhibition takes you through the entire process, from mining to cutting, sawing, shaping, faceting, polishing, and setting diamonds. There's also an extensive display of gems and semi-precious stones. Sorry, no free samples. *Address:* 10 Hanover St., W1 (0171-629-5511). *Hours:* Mon-Fri 9:30am-5:30pm, Sat 9:30am-1:30pm. **U:** Oxford Circus. **B:** 6,12, 53, 88.

21st Century London

The Architecture Foundation Gallery presents ongoing shows that explore the most avant-garde contemporary building projects in town, as well as visionary plans for the future. There are also fascinating models of London and free lectures on architecture, urban planning, and design. *Address:* 30 Bury St., SW1 (0171-839-9389). *Hours:* Tues-Fri noon-6:00pm; Sat & Sun 2:00pm-6:00pm. **U:** Piccadilly

Southwark Cathedral

South Bank

Southwark Cathedral
The oldest and finest Gothic building in London, Southwark Cathedral's current incarnation dates to 1206, when it was known as St. Mary Overie. A succession of alterations, fires, and embellishments have created an unusual but pleasing pastiche of architecture and decoration. There's a chapel dedicated to the founder of Harvard University, two Shakespeare memorials, and numerous tombs of bishops, poets, courtiers, and dramatists. Southwark makes an impressive venue for free lunchtime recitals on Monday and Tuesday. *Address:* Montague Close & Cathedral St., SE1 (0171-407-2939). *Hours:* daily 8:00am-6:00pm. **U:** London Bridge. **B:** 8A, 10, 18, 21, 35, 40, 43, 44, 48, 70, 95. **H T**

National Theatre
Denys Lasdun's daring "concrete bunker," opened in 1976, provides an exciting venue for theater, music, and art. Free attractions include Daily concerts at the Lyttelton Theatre, exhibitions of theatrical and contemporary art, lectures, readings, and terrific riverside views. *Address:* Waterloo Rd., South Bank, SE1 (0171-928-2252). *Hours:* Mon-Sat 10:00am-11:00pm. **U:** Waterloo. **B:** 1, 4, 5, 68, 70, 149, 171, 176, 188, 501. **H T**

Royal Festival Hall
Built in 1951 for the Festival of Britain, this aesthetically pleasing concert hall presents a wide range of free activities, including art shows, poetry readings, and musical performances daily from 12:30pm-2:30pm (and on Friday at 5:15pm). *Address:* Belvedere Rd., SE1 (0171-928-3002). *Hours:* daily 10:00am-10:30pm. **U:** Waterloo. **H T**

South Bank Crafts Centre

Overshadowed by the Royal Festival Hall, this center furnishes working space to craftspeople and promotes a variety of British crafts. Skilled artisans working in textiles, ceramics, precious metals, and wood demonstrate their skills and display finished pieces. *Address:* Hungerford Bridge, South Bank, SE1 (0171-928-0681). *Hours:* Tues-Sun 11:00am-7:00pm. **U:** Waterloo.

Jubilee Gardens

The riverside gardens, opened in 1977 to celebrate Queen Elizabeth II's silver jubilee, make an excellent picnic spot with a view. In the summer, frequent free concerts begin at noon. *Address:* Queen's Walk, SE1. *Hours:* daily, dawn-dusk.

Museum of Garden History

The Tradescant Trust and Museum of Garden History was founded in 1977 to save the historic St. Mary-at-Lambeth Church from demolition. The campaign resulted in this quirky operation honoring the achievements of two John Tradescants, a father and son team of royal gardeners who traveled to colonial America to collect exotic flora for Charles I's gardens. The Trust has restored the church, which now houses the world's first museum on gardening, and recreated a 17th-century garden in the churchyard, where the Tradescant tomb stands next to the grave of Captain Bligh of the *H.M.S. Bounty*. *Address:* Lambeth Palace Rd., SE1 (0171-261-1891). *Hours:* Mon-Fri 11:00am-3:00pm, Sun 10:30am-5:00pm (March-Dec). **U:** Lambeth North, Waterloo. **B:** 77, 159, 168A, 170, 507. **H T**

Lambeth Palace

Despite extensive 19th-century renovations, the 800-year-old London residence of the Archbishop of Canterbury remains essentially medieval in appearance. Within the high, crenelated walls of the red brick palace, there's the Great Hall with a superb hammer beam roof, an eerie 12th-century crypt, an excellent portrait collection, and a medieval library. *Address:* Lambeth Palace Rd., SE1 (0171-928-8282). *Hours:* tours by appointment only. **U:** Lambeth North, Waterloo. **B:** 77, 159, 168A, 170, 507. **T**

The Tradescant Garden at St. Mary-at-Lambeth Church.
(Photo: Group Three Photography Ltd.)

Imperial War Museum

The completely revamped and expanded Imperial War Museum cleverly recreates the frightening atmosphere of World War I front line conditions in the "Trench Experience," as well as the sights, sounds, and even smells of an underground air raid shelter in the "Blitz Experience." Amidst four floors of galleries and the spectacular exhibit hall, you'll find fighter aircraft, tanks, subs, artillery, uniforms, medals, and superb audio-visual exhibits. *Address:* Lambeth Rd., SE1 (0171-735-8922). *Hours:* daily 4:30pm-6:00pm. **U:** Lambeth North, Elephant & Castle, Waterloo. **B:** 1, 3, 10, 12, 44, 63, 109, 155, 159, 171, 184. **H T C**

Elizabethan Inn

The half-timbered George Inn, built in 1598, is the last galleried coaching inn remaining in London. Although the inn is owned by the National Trust, it is leased to Whitbread's Brewery and has a working pub. *Address:* 77 Borough High St., SE1 (0171-407-2056). *Hours:* Mon-Sat 11:00am-11:00pm; Sun noon-10:00pm. **U:** Borough. **B:** 133, 501.

New Caledonian Market

It's essential to arrive early if you want to find bargains at South London's most famous antiques market. The diversity of jewelry, toys, antiquarian books, ephemera, and other antiques is, as one dealer said, "positively Brobdingnagian." *Address:* Tower Bridge Rd., SE1. *Hours:* Fri 6:00am-2:00pm. **U:** Borough or London Bridge. **B:** 1, 12, 53, 188. **H**

Young Unknowns Gallery

Run by a collective of artists, this fringe gallery provides an exhibition vehicle for avant-garde artists through both eclectic and thematic shows. *Address:* 82 The Cut, SE1 (0171-928-3415). *Hours:* Mon-Fri noon-7:30pm, Sat 10:00am-3:00pm. **U:** Waterloo. **B:** 1, 12, 53, 68, 188, C1.

India Office Collection

Now a branch of the British Library, the India Office Collection has its origins in the records of the famous East India Company. The extensive collection comprises manuscripts, paintings, prints, documents, photographs, periodicals, antiques, furniture, and sculpture relating to the cultures of India and Southeast Asia.

Address: 137 Blackfriars Rd., SE1 (0171-928-9531). *Hours:* Mon-Fri 9:30am-1:00pm. **U:** Blackfriars, Waterloo. **B:** 1, 12, 68.

Maugham Theatrical Paintings Collection

Somerset Maugham bequeathed his collection of paintings on theatrical subjects to the National Theatre on the condition that the general public could view them without charge. British theater buffs will especially enjoy the portraits of great actors in their enduring triumphs. *Address:* South Bank Arts Centre, SE1 (0171-633-0880). *Hours:* Mon-Sat 10:00am-11:00pm. **U:** Waterloo. **B:** 1, 4, 5, 68, 70, 149, 501. **H**

St. George the Martyr

This handsome Georgian church has a wealth of historic and literary associations, but it's probably best known as "Little Dorrit's Church." Dickens readers will recall that the heroine of *Little Dorrit* finds refuge at St. George's and later marries there. The restored ornamental ceiling, with its gamboling cherubs, is unique in Britain. *Address:* Borough High St., SE1 (0171-405-1456). *Hours:* Mon-Fri noon-4:00pm. **U:** Borough. **B:** 8A, 10, 17, 21, 35, 40.

Platts Market

This crafts and antiques market makes an entertaining diversion if you're catching a train or simply passing through London Bridge Station. Platts is known especially for handmade items at modest prices. *Address:* Station Hall, London Bridge Underground, SE1. *Hours:* Mon-Fri 10:00am-5:00pm.

London Weekend Television

Fans of British television can obtain free tickets for tapings of their favorite shows by writing well in advance to Ticket Office, London Weekend Television, South Bank Television Centre, London, SE1.

South London Art Gallery

Established in 1868 by the celebrated artist Lord Leighton, the Gallery contains a respected collection of Victorian-era paintings, including works by Ford Madox Brown, G.F. Watts, and Leighton himself. There are also frequent temporary shows covering photography, sculpture, and textile arts. *Address:* Peckham

Rd., SE5 (0171-703-6120). *Hours:* Tues-Sat 10:00am-6:00pm,
Sun 3:00pm-6:00pm. **U:** Oval.

St. George's Cathedral

This impressive Gothic Revival Roman Catholic Cathedral was
designed by Augustus Pugin, architect of the Houses of Parliament. The interior, with its elegant, white fluted columns, is lit
by colorful stained glass windows and features an ornate carved
and gilded high altar. *Address:* Lambeth Rd., SE1 (0171-928-
5256). *Hours:* daily, 6:30am-8:00pm. **U:** Lambeth North. **B:** 10,
12, 44, 53. **T**

Hay's Galleria

The "new" London is rising from the ruined Docklands with
extraordinary revivals like this Victorianesque shopping and
entertainment complex. The old warehouses of Hay's Dock
have been retrofitted with an enormous, barrel-vaulted glass atrium and an elegant arcade. With spectacular Thames views, free
musical events, a crafts market, and fantastic fountain sculpture,
the Galleria makes a great retreat. *Address:* Tooley St., SE1
(0171-357-7770). *Hours:* daily, 7:00am-11:30pm. **U:** London
Bridge. **B:** 7A, 47, 70.

GREATER
LONDON

Highgate

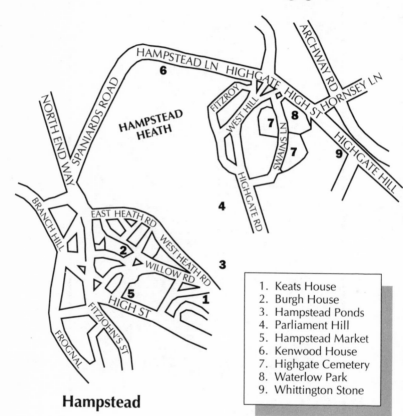

HAMPSTEAD LN HIGHGATE
NORTH END WAY
SPANIARDS ROAD
ARCHWAY RD
HORNSEY LN
HIGH ST
FITZROY
WEST HILL
HAMPSTEAD HEATH
6
SWAINS LN
HIGHGATE RD
HIGHGATE HILL
7
8
7
9
4
BRANCH HILL
EAST HEATH RD
WEST HEATH RD
2
WILLOW RD
3
5
HIGH ST
1
FITZJOHN'S ST
FROGNAL

Hampstead

1. Keats House
2. Burgh House
3. Hampstead Ponds
4. Parliament Hill
5. Hampstead Market
6. Kenwood House
7. Highgate Cemetery
8. Waterlow Park
9. Whittington Stone

Greater London

Hampstead and Highgate

Kenwood House (Iveagh Bequest)

Set on the northern ridge of Hampstead Heath, Kenwood House is a stately "country" estate just minutes from Piccadilly. In 1764, Robert Adam transformed Kenwood House from a simple brick villa into a grand, neo-classical mansion for William Murray, the Lord Chief Justice. The glory of Kenwood is indisputably the Iveagh Bequest—a collection of paintings by Rembrandt, Hals, Vermeer, Bols, Gainsborough, Turner, and Reynolds, plus the finest examples of 18th-century English furniture. The collection would grace any museum. In the summer, outdoor concerts are held at an idyllic lakeside setting. *Address:* Hampstead Lane, NW3 (0181-348-1286). *Hours:* April-Sept: daily 10:00am-6:00pm; Oct-March: daily 10:00am-4:00pm. **U:** Golders Green, Archway. **B:** 210. **H**

Hampstead Heath

You can escape the bustle of the city and feel as though you're deep in the countryside with a short trip to this 800-acre park. Probably London's most beautiful park, with vast stretches of rolling hills, woods, and unspoiled heathland, Hampstead Heath is also full of sports facilities, splendid views, gardens, and wildlife. Fairs are held there in April, May, and August, and there are free art shows on weekends June-August. *Address:* Heath Road, NW3 (0171-485-4491). *Hours:* open 24 hours. **U:** Hampstead, Golders Green. **B:** 24, 46, 168, 268. **H C**

Keats House

Hampstead Mixed Bathing Pond

Feel the need for a freshwater swim? Hampstead Pond is a bit antiquated, but it has an enduring Victorian charm, and the wooded setting is terrific. *Address:* East Heath Road, NW3 (0171-435-2366). *Hours:* May-Sept: daily 10:00am-6:00pm. **U:** Hampstead. **B:** 24, 46, 168, 268. **C**

Keats House

The Romantic poet John Keats spent his most prolific years in this simple Regency house. Opened to the public in 1925 on the 135th anniversary of Keats' birth, the extensively restored home is now a museum devoted to his life and work. *Address:* Wentworth Place, Keats Grove, NW3 (0171-435-2062). *Hours:* April-Oct: Mon-Fri 2:00pm-6:00pm, Sat 10:00am-1:00pm, Sun 2:00pm-5:00pm; Nov-March: Mon-Fri 1:00pm-5:00pm, Sat 10:00am-5:00pm, Sun 2:00pm-5:00pm. **U:** Hampstead. **B:** 24, 46, 168, 268. **T**

Burgh House

Built by Quakers in 1703, Burgh House is a fine, Queen Anne-style home now maintained as the Hampstead Museum and a cultural activities center. Displays illustrate life in old Hampstead Village, and there's an exhibit of prints by John Constable and frequent art shows. Poetry readings and music recitals are held in the delightful Music Room. *Address:* New End Square, NW3 (0171-431-0144). *Hours:* Wed-Sun noon-5:00pm. **U:** Hampstead. **B:** 24, 46, 168, 268. **T**

Hampstead Community Market

This great village market has the feel of a country flea market. The indoor stalls are full of homemade and handcrafted goods, old books, antiques, Victoriana, curios, period clothing, and old pictures. *Address:* Hampstead High St., NW3. *Hours:* Mon-Sat 9:30am-6:00pm. **U:** Hampstead.

Primrose Hill Park

On a clear day, Primrose Hill provides a superb vantage point for a panoramic view of central London. Throughout the year the wooded royal park is a venue for kite flyers, Druid rituals (on the Autumnal Equinox), holiday fireworks, and winter tobogganers. *Address:* Primrose Hill Rd., NW3 (0171-486-7905). *Hours:* open 24 hours. **U:** Camden Town, Chalk Farm. **B:** 31, 74. **C**

Camden Arts Centre

The Camden Arts Centre presents exhibitions of contemporary British and international painting, sculpture, photography, and crafts. There's also a variety of special events, courses, lectures, and discussions. *Address:* Arkwright Rd., NW3 (0171-435-2643). *Hours:* Tues-Thurs noon-8:00pm, Fri-Sun noon-6:00pm. **U:** Finchley Road.

Highgate Cemetery

Opened in 1838, the bifurcated Highgate Cemetery is London's best known and eeriest graveyard. The eastern branch is famous for the tomb of Karl Marx, who died in 1883 and is buried beneath an immense bust. The western branch is a ghostly forest of Victorian tombs, catacombs, vaults, and gravestones overgrown with creepers and ivy. *Address:* Swain's Lane, N6 (0181-340-1834). *Hours: East Branch:* April-Sept: Mon-Sat 9:00am-

5:00pm, Sun 2:00pm-5:00pm; Oct-March: Mon-Sat 9:00am-4:00pm, Sun 1:00pm-4:00pm; *West Branch:* April-Sept: daily 10:00am-4:00pm; Oct-March: daily 10:00am-3:00pm. **U:** Archway. **B:** 271.

Whittington Stone
This monument, topped with a marble cat, commemorates the celebrated four-time Lord Mayor and rat-catcher Dick Whittington. The memorial, set in 1821, marks the spot where legend says he heard the Bow Bells calling him to "turn again Whittington." *Address:* Highgate Hill, N6. **U:** Archway.

Waterlow Park
This woodsy, 26-acre park was presented to the people of Highgate Village in 1889 by the Lord Mayor of London, Sir Sydney Waterlow. Adjacent to Highgate Cemetery, the hilly park provides stunning views of the London skyline. It also has a charming aviary, a terraced rose garden, ornamental ponds, and a bandstand for free summer concerts (Sunday at 3:00pm and Thursday evenings). *Address:* Highgate High St., N6. *Hours:* daily, dawn to dusk. **U:** Highgate or Archway. **B:** 271. **H C**

Camden Town, Islington, and East End

Whitechapel Art Gallery

The turn-of-the-century Whitechapel Gallery, designed by C.H. Townsend and decorated with Arts and Crafts-style reliefs, presents changing exhibitions of contemporary and modern art. Both David Hockney and Barbara Hepworth first displayed their work at the Whitechapel. A weekly series of videos and artist-made films is presented free each Thursday at 6:30pm. *Address:* 80 Whitechapel High St., E1 (0171-377-0107). *Hours:* Tues, Thurs-Sun 11:00am-5:00pm; Wed 11:00am-8:00pm. **U:** Aldgate East. **B:** 5, 15, 25, 42, 253. **H T**

Whitechapel Market

Bustling, boisterous, and colorful, Whitechapel is a genuine neighborhood market, where the stall-holders will take the time to chat even if you're not buying. Running along Whitechapel Road between Valence Road and Brady Street, the market's stalls sell everything from books to baked goods. *Address:* Whitechapel Road, E1. *Hours:* Mon-Sat 8:30am-5:00pm. **U:** Whitechapel, Stepney Green.

Stepping Stone Farm

A working farm in the midst of the East End may seem a bit incongruous, but Stepping Stone is just one example of these popular urban-agrarian enterprises in Britain. Kids will enjoy a break from culture-cruising at this four-acre mini-farm with its friendly ponies, goats, mules, pigs, and lambs. *Address:* Stepney Way, E1. *Hours:* daily, 10:00am-5:00pm. **U:** Stepney Green. **C**

A craftsman pours pewter at Englefields.

Metropolitan Police Thames Division Museum

The displays at this unusual museum date from 1798—when the Thames Marine Police was chartered—and include relics of notorious East End murder cases, uniforms, paintings, and documents. *Address:* 98 Wapping High St., E1 (0171-488-5391). *Hours:* Mon-Fri, 8:00am-4:00pm (by appointment). **U:** Wapping. **B:** 40, 42, 67.

Geffrye Museum

Set in a row of early 18th-century almshouses, the museum is named for its benefactor, Sir Robert Geffrye, Lord Mayor of London in 1685 and Master of the Ironmongers Guild. Today the almshouses contain a chronological series of period room settings exploring London lifestyles from Elizabethan times to the 1950's. There's also a real Georgian street, complete with stores and an 18th-century woodworker's shop. *Address:* Kingsland Rd., E2 (0171-739-9893). *Hours:* Tues-Sat 10:00am-5:00pm; Sun 2:00pm-5:00pm. **U:** Old Street, Bethnal Green. **B:** 48, 67, 149, 243. **H T C**

Crown & Rose Pewter

Making pewter is a 300-year-old craft. You can take a step back in time by visiting Englefields' Crown & Rose pewter workshops, where pewter is produced by the same methods and molds used by the company's artisans for three centuries. *Address:* Cheshire St., E2 (0171-739-3616). *Tours:* Tues, Wed, Thurs at 10:30am. **U:** Bethnal Green, Liverpool St. **B:** 6, 22, 48, 55, 78. **T**

London Buddhist Centre

This East End center offers free introductory meditation courses and educational classes on the various schools of Buddhism. *Address:* 51 Roman Rd., E2 (0181-981-1225). *Hours:* Mon-Fri 10:15am-5:00pm. **U:** Bethnal Green.

Chisenhale Gallery

Politically-oriented art is the mainstay at this enormous studio/gallery complex. Lectures and discussion groups meet daily. *Address:* 64 Chisenhale Rd., E3 (0181-981-4518). *Hours:* Wed-Sun 1:00pm-6:00pm. **U:** Bethnal Green. **B:** 8, 8A, 277. **H T**

Ragged Schools Museum

The Ragged Schools were founded in 1870 to provide free education and food for London's poor children. The museum, housed in converted canal-side warehouses, was the first of 30 branch schools. There's a reconstructed classroom, a recreation of a Victorian sweatshop, antiques, and displays on life in the East End. *Address:* 46-48 Copperfield Rd., E3 (0181-980-6405). *Hours:* Mon-Fri 10:00am-5:00pm. **U:** Mile End. **B:** 25, 106.

Christchurch
The triangular spire of this Hawksmoor-designed church has dominated Spitalfields for 250 years. Ongoing restoration aims at rejuvenation of the lofty classical interior. Regularly scheduled free concerts should return following renovations. *Address:* Commercial St., E1 (0171-247-7202). *Hours:* Mon-Fri, 10:00am-5:00pm. **U:** Aldgate East. **B:** 8A, 22, 35, 47, 48.

East London Mosque
This mosque is an ingenious architectural blend of contemporary design and traditional Middle Eastern themes. Ironically, an Orthodox synagogue once stood on the site. *Address:* 84 Whitechapel Road, E1 (0171-247-1357). *Hours:* daily, 9:00am-9:00pm. **U:** Whitechapel, Aldgate East. **B:** 5, 15, 25, 40, 253, 510.

Petticoat Lane Market
The largest and most famous Sunday market in London has an amazing array of jewelry, leather goods, antiques, curios, and just plain junk. Get there early — the best buys are gone by 10:00am. *Address:* Middlesex St., E1. *Hours:* Sun 6:00am-2:00pm. **U:** Liverpool St., Aldgate, Aldgate East.

Brick Lane Market
Less famous than nearby Petticoat Lane Market, this is a real East End flea market. Chaotic and colorful, stalls spill into connecting streets and courtyards, with traders selling everything from knick-knacks to smoked salmon. *Address:* Brick Lane, E1. *Hours:* Sun 6:00am-2:00pm. **U:** Liverpool St.

Queen Mary College Museum of Geology
Rockhounds won't want to miss this teaching and research museum specializing in the geology of the British Isles. *Address:* Mile End Road, E1 (0181-980-4811). *Hours:* Mon-Fri 9:00am-5:00pm. **U:** Mile End.

Bethnal Green Museum of Childhood

This branch of the Victoria and Albert Museum presents Europe's greatest collection of toys, games, dolls, children's books, bears, puppets, and doll houses. Each Christmas there's an exciting seasonal display; temporary exhibitions are held year-round. *Address:* Cambridge Heath Rd., E2 (0181-980-3204). *Hours:* Mon-Thurs & Sat 10:00am-6:00pm; Sun 2:30pm-6:00pm. **U:** Bethnal Green. **B:** 8, 8A, 106. **C**

Tobacco Dock

Tobacco Dock Village and the 24 acres of vaults beneath were built from 1811-1814 to house hogsheads of tobacco and casks of spirits. In 1989, a modern shopping and entertainment complex opened in the renovated warehouses and elegantly curved vaults. Tobacco Dock celebrates many holidays with special events, concerts, and craft demonstrations. Daily free entertainment of every kind—from puppet shows to classical recitals—contribute to the Covent Garden-like atmosphere. *Address:* Wapping Lane, E1 (0171-702-9681). *Hours:* daily 10:00am-11:00pm. **U:** Wapping or Shadwell (DLR). **B:** 15, 25, 42, 78, 100, 510, or Docklands Minibus. **H C**

St. George-in-the-East

Built in 1711, St. George's was designed by Hawksmoor and has his trademark tower with pepper-pot turrets. Gutted by Nazi incendiaries in 1941, it was restored in 1964 and today remains one of London's greatest churches. *Address:* The Highway, E1 (0171-481-1345). *Hours:* Tues-Sun 8:00am-5:00pm. **U:** Shadwell. **B:** 5, 15, 25, 42, 78.

Camerawork

This innovative workshop and exhibition space presents monthly photo shows and touring exhibitions, as well as courses, talks, workshops, and special events. *Address:* 121 Roman Rd., E2 (0181-980-6256). *Hours:* Tues-Fri 1:00pm-6:00pm; Sat 1:00pm-3:00pm. **U:** Bethnal Green. **B:** 8, 8A, 106. **H**

Business Design Centre

After use as a site for cattle shows, revival meetings, bullfights, military tournaments, and the annual Cruft's Dog Show, the tremendous iron and glass Royal Agricultural Hall has a new life as the Business Design Centre. This commercial trade center presents weekly exhibitions on interior design and displays innovative new products from Common Market manufacturers. *Address:* 52 Upper St., N1 (0171-359-3535). *Hours:* Mon-Fri 9:00am-5:30pm. **U:** Angel. **B:** 19, 30, 43. **H**

Camden Passage

The Passage, a quaint Dickensian alley, is thick with curio, antique, and bric-a-brac shops. On Wednesdays and Saturdays, the Passage and adjoining streets become a colorful flea market. There are also several indoor arcades with small shops specializing in art nouveau objects, militaria, porcelain, books, jewelry, and glass. *Address:* off Upper St., N1. *Market Hours:* Wed and Sat 8:00am-5:00pm. *Shop Hours:* Tues-Sat 9:00am-5:00pm. **U:** Angel. **B:** 19, 30, 43.

Union Chapel

Inspired by the Church of Santa Fosca in Venice, Italy, Thomas Cubitt designed the dramatic Union Chapel. Americans will be impressed by the piece of Plymouth Rock on display, donated to the church in 1883 by the Pilgrim Society. *Address:* Compton Terrace, N1 (0171-354-3631). *Hours:* daily by appointment. **U:** Highbury & Islington. **B:** 4, 19, 30. **T**

Black Art Gallery

The Black Art Gallery was Britain's first non-commercial public gallery devoted to and run by black artists. Along with exhibitions of sculpture, painting, and crafts, the gallery promotes plays, concerts, poetry readings, courses, and workshops. *Address:* 227 Seven Sisters Rd., N4 (0171-263-1918). *Hours:* Tues-Sat 11:00am-7:00pm. **U:** Finsbury Park.

Freightliners City Farm

Following Islington's long agricultural tradition, Freightliners City Farm offers a working farm environment with activities for all ages—right in the heart of London! *Address:* Sheringham Rd., N7 (0171-607-0467). *Hours:* daily, 8:30am-5:00pm. **U:** Highbury & Islington. **B:** 4, 19, 30. **H C**

Regent's Canal Information Centre

Running for eight miles from Little Venice to the Limehouse Docks, Regent's Canal provides an unparalleled perspective on the historical and architectural potpourri of London. The recently opened Canal Information Centre, set in the former lock-keeper's cottage of Camden Lock, provides data on all things related to the canal, plus maps, brochures, and advice on walks and canal boat trips. *Address:* Camden Lock, NW1 (0171-482-0523). *Hours:* daily, 10:00am-5:00pm. **U:** Camden Town, Chalk Farm. **B:** 24, 29, 168.

Camden Lock Market
Although current redevelopment schemes threaten to expunge the 1960's-style funkiness of Camden Lock, its élan and energy make this market a weekend mecca for young Londoners. Once a timber wharf, Camden Lock has become the nucleus of an arts, crafts, and entertainment center with a counter-culture flavor. All manner of Third World clothing, music, homemade foods, and crafts are on sale, along with jewelry, musical instruments, ceramics, leatherwork, bric-a-brac, posters, books, period clothing, and contemporary accoutrement. *Address:* Camden High St., NW1 (0171-485-4457). *Hours:* Sat & Sun 8:00am-6:00pm. **U:** Camden Town, Chalk Farm Road. **B:** 24, 29, 168, 253. **C**

Cecil Sharp House
The historic, canal-side Cecil Sharp House is now dedicated to the promotion of traditional English folk arts, music, and dance. *Address:* 2 Regent's Park Road, NW1 (0171-485-2206). *Hours:* Mon-Fri 9:30am-5:00pm. **U:** Camden Town. **B:** 74. **T**

Artsline
This organization for the physically disabled provides information on cultural and entertainment events in Greater London, accessibility data, and a free magazine called *Disability Arts in London. Address:* 5 Crowndale Rd., NW1 (0171-388-2227). *Hours:* Mon-Fri 10:00am-5:30pm. **U:** Mornington Crescent. **B:** 24, 29, 68, 253.

St. Pancras Old Church
Built on 4th-century foundations, St. Pancras is one of Britain's oldest Christian sites. The present church is primarily 13th century, with extensive mid-19th century alterations. According to legend, Percy Bysshe Shelly first met Mary Wollstonecraft, who became his wife and wrote *Frankenstein,* in the gloomy St. Pancras graveyard. *Address:* St. Pancras Way, NW1 (0171-387-

Sunbathers in Regent's Park. (BTA photo)

7301). *Hours:* Tues-Sat 2:00pm-7:00pm, Sun 9:30am-11:00am.
U: Camden Town.

Old Stables Market
The atmospheric old barns and courtyards of this weekend market overflow with inexpensive bygones, military surplus, handicrafts, period clothing, china, curios, books, and glassware. *Address:* Chalk Farm Road, NW1. *Hours:* Sat & Sun 8:00am-6:00pm. **U:** Chalk Farm, Camden Town. **B:** 24, 28, 31, 68.

Regent's Park
This 470-acre Royal park was originally enclosed by Henry VIII as a personal hunting reserve. Today, Regent's is one of London's loveliest and liveliest public retreats. It contains one of the finest rose gardens in the world, the London Zoo, a boating lake, a bandstand for free summer concerts, a puppet theater, and assorted sports facilities, all surrounded by handsome Regency terraces, Palladian mansions, imposing gateways, and the Regent's Canal. *Address:* Inner Circle, NW1 (0171-486-7905). *Hours:* daily, 6:00am-dusk. **U:** Regent's Park, Camden Town, Baker Street, Great Portland St. **B:** 1, 2B, 13, 18, 27, 30, 74, 113, 135, 159, 176. **H C**

Mudchute City Farm
This urban farm gets its name from the silted mud dredged from the Docklands and piped into settling beds, which eventually

became grassed-over. Today, the 35-acre farm provides inner-city kids a taste of the countryside, with farm animals, gardens, orchards, and even pony rides. *Address:* Pier St., Isle of Dogs, E14 (0171-515-5901). *Hours:* April-Oct: daily, 8:00am-6:30pm; Nov-March: daily, 8:00am-5:00pm. **U:** Mudchute, Island Gardens (DLR). **B:** D7, 277, P14. **C**

Docklands Light Railway Visitor's Centre

Set in Island Gardens Park with a fabulous view of Greenwich across the Thames, the Visitor's Centre provides information on the Light Railway and on the entire Docklands development. They also have free maps and brochures, videos, and booking for Docklands tours. *Address:* Limeharbour, E14 (0171-515-3000). *Hours:* daily,10:00am-4:00pm. **U:** Island Gardens (DLR). **B:** D7, P14, 277.

St. Anne's Limehouse

This Hawksmoor-designed Baroque church was built between 1712 and 1730. Faithfully restored after WWII bomb damage, St. Anne's, with its immense tower, remains a Docklands landmark. It also has a fantastic organ built for the Great Exhibition of 1851. *Address:* Three Colt St., E14 (0171-987-1502). *Hours:* daily, 9:00am-5:00pm. **U:** Limehouse, Westferry (DLR). **B:** 5, 15, 40, 86, 106, 277, D3.

National Museum of Labour History

Opened in 1964 in the Old Limehouse Town Hall, this colorful museum presents an in-depth retrospective on the development of organized labor in Great Britain. Some of the unusual exhibits include Thomas Paine's death mask, personal memorabilia of the anarchist Kropotkin, and famous strike banners. *Address:* Commercial Rd., E14 (0171-515-3229). *Hours:* Tues-Sat 9:30am-5:00pm, Sun 2:30pm-5:30pm. **U:** Limehouse, Westferry (DLR). **B:** 5, 15, 40, 86, 106, 278.

Island History Trust

The Island History Trust has an outstanding collection of photographs, documents, and artwork illustrating the unique social life on the Isle of Dogs from the 19th century to today. *Address:* Roserton St., E14 (0171-987-6041). *Hours:* Tues-Fri 1:00pm-4:30pm. **U:** Crossharbour (DLR). **B:** D3, D5, D6, P14, 277.

National Centre for Crafts

Some of Britain's best and most original crafts are on display at the new National Centre for Crafts in Islington. Along with a terrific gallery, you'll find workshops, a library, an information center, and a crafts shop. *Address:* 44 Pentonville Rd., N1 (0171-278-7700). *Hours:* Tues-Sat 11:00am-6:00pm, Sun 2:00pm-6:00pm. **U:** Angel.

Passmore Edwards Museum

This charming museum, founded at the turn of the century, is dedicated to the preservation of the local culture, heritage, and environment of East London and the county of Essex. The museum reopened in 1990 with new displays on archaeology, history, geology, biology, and conservation. *Address:* Romford Rd., E15 (0181-519-4296). *Hours:* Wed-Fri 11:00am-5:00pm, Sat & Sun 1:00pm-5:00pm. **U:** Stratford. **B:** 10, 25, 69, 86. **C T**

North Woolwich Old Station Museum

The elegant North Woolwich Station, faithfully restored to its Victorian grandeur, now tells the story of London's railways. Fascinating indoor and outdoor exhibits explain the principles of steam locomotion and the history of the Great Eastern Railway. There are models, photographs, railway relics, and a reconstructed ticket office, but the true centerpiece of the museum is the 1876 "Coffee Pot" steam locomotive. Anyone who loves trains won't want to miss this museum! *Address:* Pier Rd., E16 (0171-474-7244). *Hours:* Mon-Wed & Sat 10:00am-5:00pm, Sun 2:00pm-5:00pm. **U:** North Woolwich (BR). **B:** 69, 101, 262, 276. **H T C**

Newham City Farm

Urban farmsteads are an inspired British phenomenon, created to provide inner-city kids an experience of rural life. Newham Farm has the requisite animals and aromas that offer a real sense of the country—all without leaving the East End. *Address:* Stansfeld Rd., E16 (0171-476-1170). *Hours:* daily, 8:00am-5:00pm. **U:** Custom House (BR). **B:** D2, 173, 262, 262A, X15. **C**

Interpretive Centre & Nature Reserve

Centered around a marvelous 12th-century Norman church, the nine-acre St. Mary Magdalene churchyard has been transformed into an urban nature preserve. There are nature trails, an interesting interpretive center, and many species of birds, animals, and plants. *Address:* Norman Rd., E6 (0181-470-4525). *Hours:* Reserve: Mon-Fri 9:00am-5:00pm, Sat & Sun 2:00pm-5:00pm; Interpretive Centre: Tues, Thurs, Sat, & Sun 2:00pm-5:00pm. **U:** East Ham. **B:** D2, 101, 104, 173. **H T C**

Shree Nathji Sanatan Hindu Temple

This is one of Britain's largest Hindu places of worship, with two central halls and four elaborate shrines to Shiva, Krishna, Rama, and Durga. *Address:* 159 Whipps Cross Rd., E11 (0181-969-7539). *Hours:* daily, 8:15am-8:00pm. **U:** Leytonstone. **B:** 257.

William Morris Gallery

Architect, poet, painter, printer, designer, and social reformer, William Morris was a central and controversial figure in both the Arts and Crafts and Socialist movements. His childhood home, known as "Water House," now contains a diverse exhibition of his works in stained glass, ceramics, textiles, furniture, and paper. The gallery also houses other period works, including pre-Raphaelite paintings, sculpture by Rodin, Rossetti, and Sickert, and ceramics by William de Morgan. *Address:* Lloyd Park, Forest Rd., E17 (0181-527-3782). *Hours:* Tues-Sat 10:00am-1:00pm & 2:00pm-5:00pm. **U:** Walthamstow Central. **B:** 34, 48, 97,123. **T**

Vestry House

In a tranquil, village-like setting surprisingly close to the busy Walthamstow town center, this quaint parish workhouse dating from 1730 contains one of London's best local history museums. Exhibits illustrate lifestyles in the Waltham Forest from Stone Age settlement to the present, with displays on archaeology, crafts, home life, costumes, and work. You'll also find Britain's first motor car — the locally built Bremer from 1894 — and a jail cell from 1840, when Vestry House contained the local hoosegow. *Address:* Vestry Rd., E17 (0181-509-1917). *Hours:* Mon-Sat 10:00am-5:00pm. **U:** Walthamstow Central. **B:** 34, 69, 97, 212. **T**

Arsenal Stadium

You don't have to be an Arsenal Football Club fan (or even know who the "Gunners" are, for that matter) to enjoy the free guided tour of Arsenal Stadium. The tour, which lasts nearly two hours, takes you behind the scenes, through the locker rooms and around the field. By the time you leave, you'll be an expert on British football lore. *Address:* Avenell Rd., N5 (0171-226-0304). *Hours:* Mon-Fri 10:00am-noon, by appointment. **U:** Arsenal. **C**

Greenwich, Blackheath, and Bromley

Royal Naval College
Designed in 1698 by Sir Christopher Wren, who incorporated sections of Greenwich Palace, this former naval hospital was completed over the next century by Vanbrugh, Hawksmoor, Ripley, and Campbell. The magnificent Baroque Painted Hall, the work of James Thornhill, was where Nelson lay in state in 1805. Facing it, the superb Wren Chapel is a rococo riot in Wedgwood pastels. *Address:* King William Walk, SE10 (0181-858-2154). *Hours:* daily 2:30pm-5:00pm. **U:** Maze Hill (BR) or Island Gardens (DLR). **B:** 177, 180, 286.

Greenwich Market
If you visit Greenwich on the weekend, be sure to stop by the popular street market. Specialties there include crafts, home-made food, antiques, clothing, books, and gifts. *Address:* Market Square, SE10. *Hours:* Sat & Sun 9:00am-5:00pm. **U:** Greenwich (BR). **B:** 177, 180, 286.

Greenwich Park
Established in 1433, Greenwich is the oldest enclosed Royal park in Britain. In the 1660's, Le Notre, the landscaper of Versailles, redesigned the park for Charles II. Rising 155 feet above the Thames, the park features sweeping panoramas around London. Included within its 200 acres are a deer park, bird sanctuary, the Old Royal Observatory, the Wolfe Monument, and Bronze Age tumuli. During the summer, there are free puppet shows and band concerts. *Address:* King William Walk, SE10 (0181-858-2608). *Hours:* daily, 5:00am-sunset. **U:** Greenwich (BR). **B:** 177,180,286. **H C**

St. Alfege's
Nicholas Hawksmoor built this elegant church in 1711 to replace a succession of churches on the site since Alfege, the

Archbishop of Canterbury, was martyred there by Danish invaders in 1012. Murals by James Thornhill and carvings by Grinling Gibbons grace the interior. *Address:* Church St. & Greenwich High Rd., SE10 (0181-858-3458). *Hours:* Mon & Wed-Fri 11:00am-5:00pm, Sat & Sun 2:00pm-4:00pm. **U:** Greenwich (BR). **B:** 177, 180, 286.

Greenwich Antique Market

Get here early on Saturday for the best bargains in small antiques and bygones. Among the goodies you'll find at this indoor market are Victorian jewelry, antiquarian books, porcelain, and art nouveau baubles. *Address:* Greenwich High Rd., SE10. *Hours:* Sat (and Sunday in summer) 8:00am-4:00pm. **U:** Greenwich (BR). **B:** 177, 180, 286.

Ranger's House

This early 18th-century mansion acquired its name in 1815 when it became the official residence of the Greenwich Park Ranger. Converted in 1974 to an art museum, it now houses the Suffolk Collection of Jacobean and Royal Portraits. There's also the notable Dolmetsch Collection of historic musical instruments and a fine selection of 17th- and 18th-century English furniture. Chamber concerts and poetry readings are offered year-round. *Address:* Chesterfield Walk, SE10 (0181-853-0035). *Hours:* daily, 10:00am-5:00pm. **U:** Blackheath (BR). **B:** 53, 54, 75. **H T**

Eltham Palace

The ancient Eltham Palace, with foundations nearly 1,000 years old, was a favorite of English royalty until Henry VIII forsook it for nearby Greenwich Palace. The venerable old buildings fell into decay until 1931, when the Great Hall was restored. The hall, 101 feet long by 36 feet wide, dates from the early 15th century and has a nonpareil hammer beam roof and wonderfully grotesque carvings. *Address:* off Court Yard Rd., SE9 (0181-859-2112). *Hours:* April-Oct: Thurs & Sun 11:00am-7:00pm; Nov-March: Thurs & Sun 11:00am-4:00pm. **U:** Eltham (BR). **B:** 21A, 108, 124A, 126, 160, 228, B1.

Avery Hill Winter Garden

Built in 1890 by the owner of Avery Hill Estate, the Winter Garden has 750 species of plants in cold, temperate, and tropical greenhouses—a collection second only to Kew Gardens. The surrounding park has 19 acres of gardens and plant nurseries. *Address:* Avery Hill, SE9 (0181-850-3217). *Hours:* Mon-Fri 1:00pm-4:00pm, Sat & Sun 11:00am-6:00pm. **U:** Eltham. **H**

Charlton House

Charlton House has been described as London's finest Jacobean house. Built in 1607 for Prince Henry's tutor, Dean Adam Newton, the H-shaped, red brick manor house has superb plasterwork, unusual woodwork, and eccentric fireplaces and chimney pieces. *Address:* Charlton Rd., SE7 (0181-856-3951). *Hours:* Mon-Fri 9:00am-5:00pm. **U:** Maze Hill or Blackheath (BR).

Morden College

This little-known gem by Wren was commissioned in 1695 as an almshouse by Sir John Morden, a wealthy importer. The collegiate-style quadrangle, with its ornamental stone gateway, is still used as a home for the elderly and is set in a lovely, 18th-century park. *Address:* 19 St. Germain's Place, SE10 (0181-858-3365). *Hours:* Mon-Sat 11:00am-3:00pm (by appointment). **U:** Blackheath (BR). **B:** 21, 61, 126, 132. **T**

Museum of Artillery

Housed in the Rotunda, a John Nash architectural novelty built in 1814 to celebrate Napoleon's abdication, the Museum of Artillery was founded by General William Congreve in 1778. The chronologically arranged exhibits trace the development of the cannon from the 14th to 20th centuries. A film describes how artillery pieces are produced, and there's an extensive display of small arms from 1500 to the present. *Address:* Repository Rd., SE18 (0181-316-5402). *Hours:* April-Oct: Mon-Fri noon-5:00pm, Sat & Sun 1:00pm-5:00pm; Nov-March: Mon-Fri noon-4:00pm, Sat & Sun 1:00pm-4:00pm. **U:** Woolwich Dockyard (BR). **H T**

Royal Artillery Regimental Museum

This museum illustrates the heroic history of the Royal Artillery from its formation in 1716 through the Falklands War, with displays of weapons, medals, uniforms, paintings, and various militaria. The museum is based in the Old Royal Military Academy, built in 1741. *Address:* Academy Rd., SE18 (0181-854-2242). *Hours:* Mon-Fri 12:30pm-4:30pm, Sat & Sun 2:00pm-5:00pm. **U:** Woolwich Arsenal (BR). **B:** 161, 126, 122. **T**

Greenwich Borough Museum

This museum's collections focus on the natural and human history of Greenwich, Woolwich, and Plumstead. Local archaeological displays include important finds from Lesnes Abbey. *Address:* 232 Plumstead High St., SE18 (0181-855-3240). *Hours:* Mon 2:00pm-8:00pm, Tues-Sat 10:00am-5:00pm. **U:** Plumstead (BR).

Woodlands Art Gallery and History Centre

Woodlands was erected in 1774 as a country estate for John Julius Angerstein, whose personal collection of Old Masters formed the foundation of the National Gallery. The art gallery has a large collection of 18th- and 19th-century watercolors and presents monthly shows. The History Centre holds an extensive collection of photos, maps, and documents relating to London history. *Address:* 90 Mycenae Rd., SE3 (0181-858-4631). *Hours:* Mon, Tues, Thurs, & Fri 10:00am-7:30pm, Sat 10:00am-6:00pm, Sun 2:00pm-6:00pm. **U:** Westcombe Park (BR). **B:** 54, 75.

London Borough of Bromley Museum

Occupying a medieval manor house, the Bromley Museum was built on the wide-ranging archaeology and ethnography collections of Baron Avebury. A close friend of Charles Darwin, Avebury accumulated a vast hoard of antiquities during his global travels. Displays range from the Stone Age to the early 20th century and include Roman and Saxon jewelry, coins, pottery, clothing, and ceremonial objects. *Address:* The Priory, Church Hill, BR6 (0689-31551). *Hours:* Mon-Sat 9:00am-6:00pm. **U:** Orpington (BR). **H T C**

Hall Place

Hall Place, a 15th-century Tudor stone mansion, is set within exquisitely landscaped gardens. The restored house is now home to the Bexley Borough Museum, which presents permanent exhibitions on British archaeology, geology, and natural history, along with changing shows on London social history. The magnificent grounds, with topiary displays, heather, herb, rose, and rock gardens, and conservatory collections, make Hall Place well worth the trip from central London. *Address:* Bourne Rd., Bexley (0322-526574). *Hours:* House: Mon-Sat 10:00am-5:00pm; Gardens: Mon-Fri 7:30am-sunset, Sat & Sun 9:00am-sunset. **U:** Bexley (BR). **H T**

Brixton and South London

London Glassblowing Workshop

The London Glassblowing Workshop is famous for its colorful, fanciful pieces. You can watch the bulging cheeks of master glassblowers at work in the shop and be awed by the finished pieces at their nearby gallery. *Address:* Weston St., SE1 (0171-403-2800). *Hours:* Mon-Fri 11:00am-5:00pm **U:** Rotherhithe. **B:** 47, 70, 70A, 188.

Lavender Pond Pump House

This Victorian pump house has been refurbished to house an ecological educational center and local environmental museum. There's also a small, attractive nature reserve. *Address:* Lavender Rd., Rotherhithe St., SE16 (0171-232-0498). *Hours:* Mon-Fri 9:00am-3:00pm. **U:** Rotherhithe. **B:** 47, 47A, 70. **H C**

St. Mary's

Though a church has stood on this site since Saxon days, the present brick building with its octagonal obelisk spire dates from 1715. Inside, the wooden barrel roof rests on huge pillars — actually tree trunks encased in plaster. The lovely altar is decorated with rich carvings by the prolific Grinling Gibbons. Christopher Jones, captain of the *Mayflower,* was buried in the churchyard. His grave disappeared during 18th-century rebuilding, but a monument was erected to Jones in 1965. *Address:* St. Marychurch Street, SE16 (0171-231-2465). *Hours:* Mon-Sat 8:30am-4:00pm. **U:** Rotherhithe.

Livesey Museum

The Livesey Museum was built in 1890 to house the Camberwell Public Library. In 1974, the charming Victorian building was opened as a venue for exhibitions on the South London community. *Address:* 682 Old Kent Rd., SE15 (0171-639-5604). *Hours:* Mon-Sat 10:00am-5:00pm. **U:** Surrey Docks. **B:** 21, 53, 78, 141, 177, P5. **C**

Surrey Docks Farm
Surrey Docks Farm recently relocated to a Thames-side location, where kids of all ages can get hands-on experience with all kinds of farm animals. *Address:* 1 South Wharf, Rotherhithe St., SE16 (0171-231-1010). *Hours:* daily, 8:30am-5:00pm. **U:** Rotherhithe or Surrey Docks. **B:** 47, 70, 70A. **C**

Cuming Museum
This eclectic museum grew from the personal collection begun by Richard Cuming in 1782. Acquired by the Borough of Southwark in 1902, the diverse collection incorporates Roman finds, pilgrims' badges from the Middle Ages, Dickens's personal mementos, and a fun exhibit on a family dairy that operated in the neighborhood for nearly two centuries. A special feature of the Cuming is the thoroughly bizarre Lovett Collection of Charms and Amulets, which explores superstition through the ages. *Address:* 155 Walworth Rd., SE17 (0171-703-3324, ext. 32). *Hours:* Mon-Sat 10:00am-5:30pm. **U:** Elephant & Castle. **T**

Crystal Palace Park
Only the foundations remain of the Crystal Palace, a gigantic, cathedral-like structure in iron and glass designed by Joseph Paxton to house the Great Exhibition of 1851. When the exhibition ended, the Crystal Palace was removed from its Hyde Park site and placed on Syndenham Hill in South London, where it was a popular entertainment center until destroyed by fire in 1936. Today, there's a major sports complex and park, with a children's zoo, boating lake, and 20 life-size dinosaur replicas built in 1854. Free concerts run May-Sept. *Address:* Norwood, SE19 (0181-676-0700). *Hours:* daily, 8:00am-dusk. **U:** Crystal Palace (BR). **B:** 3, 63, 122, 137, 157, 227, 249. **H T C**

Horniman Museum
The remarkable art nouveau façade will alert you to expect an unusual museum. The splendid building, designed by C.H. Townsend, is home to the truly eccentric personal collections of tea magnate Frederick J. Horniman. Opened in 1901, the museum explores anthropology, natural history, ethnography, and

music with quintessentially English verve and ebullience. This is one museum even the kids will love. *Address:* London Rd., SE23 (0181-699-2339). *Hours:* Mon-Sat 10:30am-6:00pm, Sun 2:00pm-6:00pm. **U:** Forest Hill (BR). **B:** 12, 12A, 63, 122, 124, 176, 185. **C T**

Horniman Gardens

A delightful 11-acre garden surrounds the Horniman Museum. There's a children's zoo, a rose garden, a rock garden, a nature trail, a horticultural center, and a bandstand for free summer concerts on Sundays. *Address:* 100 London Rd., SE23 (0181-699-4911). *Hours:* daily, 7:00am-dusk. **H C**

Vintage Wireless Museum

In 1974, Gerald Wells opened his personal collection of vintage radios to the public. Since then, his exhibition has become an international headquarters for radio enthusiasts. Each radio, dating from 1917 to 1946, works and is displayed in 1930's-style radio shops. *Address:* 23 Rosendale Rd., SE21 (0181-670-3667) *Hours:* Mon-Sat 11:00am-7:00pm. **U:** West Dulwich (BR). **B:** 2, 3. **H T**

Black Cultural Archives Museum

This museum imaginatively explores the history of African peoples in Britain, from the Roman invasion to the present. Frequently changing exhibitions cover the full range of Afro-British culture, with emphasis on dance, graphic arts, literature, and music. *Address:* 378 Coldharbour Lane, SW9 (0171-733-3044). *Hours:* Mon-Fri 9:30am-3:30pm. **U:** Brixton. **B:** 3, 95, 109, 133, 196.

Brixton Market

Brixton is famous for its exciting Afro-Caribbean street market, where business is conducted to a constant reggae beat and the tantalizing aromas of spicy, homemade delicacies. You'll find great buys on colorful African and West Indian fabrics, clothing, and crafts, plus all kinds of records and tapes from soca to London hip-hop, inexpensive leather goods, and, of course, fabulous food. *Address:* Electric Ave. & Brixton Station Rd., SW9. *Hours:* Mon-Sat 8:00am-late afternoon. **U:** Brixton. **B:** 3, 95, 109, 133, 159, 196.

Brixton Artists' Collective

This multi-ethnic collective presents some of London's most stimulating and provocative art exhibitions. They also publish posters and postcards by member artists. *Address:* 35 Brixton Rd., SW9 (0171-733-6957). *Hours:* Mon-Sat 10:00am-6:00pm. **U:** Brixton. **B:** 3, 95, 109, 133, 159, 196.

Brixton Recreation Centre

No membership is required to enjoy this diverse leisure center. Facilities include three swimming pools, a gym, basketball courts, solarium, sauna, aerobics and yoga classes, sports halls, an indoor climbing course, and trampolines. (Some activities charge a small fee.) *Address:* Brixton Station Rd., SW9 (0171-274-7774). *Hours:* daily, 9:00am-10:00pm. **U:** Brixton. **B:** 3, 95, 109, 133, 159, 196. **C**

Northcote Road Antiques Market

This covered market houses dealers selling a wide array of antique glassware, jewelry, porcelain, toys, china, and silverware, with an emphasis on Art Deco objects. *Address:* 155 Northcote Rd., SW11 (0171-228-6850). *Hours:* Mon-Sat 10:00am-6:00pm, Sun 1:00pm-5:00pm. **U:** Clapham Junction. **B:** 49.

Battersea Arts Centre

The Battersea Arts Centre is an exciting venue for monthly exhibitions of photography, painting, and sculpture, as well as contemporary, classical, and folk music concerts. *Address:* 176 Lavender Hill, SW11 (0171-223-6557). *Hours:* daily, 10:00am-10:00pm. **U:** Clapham South. **B:** 45, 77, 156. **H C**

Battersea Park

Until the mid-19th century, this interesting Thames-side park was a marshy, wild area popular for pigeon hunting and duels. Today, the 200-acre park incorporates a children's zoo, a tropical garden, a deer park, a wildflower garden, waterfront sculpture by Henry Moore and Barbara Hepworth, herb gardens, and the ornate Peace Pagoda. The park is also a busy South London venue for fairs, races, and all kinds of special events. *Address:* Battersea Park Rd., SW9 (0181-871-7543). *Hours:* daily, dawn-dusk. **U:** Battersea Park (BR). **B:** 19, 39, 44, 45, 49, 130, 131, 170. **H C**

National Book League Collections

The unique National Book League promotes British literature of all kinds and offers advice to writers and readers alike. The League's collections include 18th- and 19th-century illustrations and engravings, the Perez Collection of Bookplates, and thousands of books on the book trade. The NBL also houses the Centre for Children's Books, Britain's only specialized center for children's literature. The Centre holds a copy of every children's book published in the U.K. and displays original illustrations from award-winning books. *Address:* 45 East Hill, SW18 (0181-8709055). *Hours:* Mon-Fri 9:00am-5:00pm. **U:** Wandsworth Town (BR). **T C**

The Rookery

This exquisite three-acre garden once surrounded a 17th-century South London mansion. There are splendid old cedars, wildflower gardens, a water garden, and the lovely, walled White Garden. *Address:* Streatham Common, SW16 (0181-769-7634). *Hours:* daily, 9:00am-sunset. **U:** Streatham (BR).

Historic Gallery

Established in 1817, the Dulwich Picture Gallery was Britain's first museum built for the purpose of displaying art. The exceptional Neo-Classical gallery was designed by the eccentric architect Sir John Soane (see page 31) a decade before the opening of the National Gallery. This pioneering museum contains a treasure trove of Old Masters, including paintings by Rubens, Van Dyck, Rembrandt, Watteau, Canaletto, Gainsborough, Ruysdael, and Tiepolo. *Address:* College Rd., SE21 (0181-693-5254). *Hours:* Fri, 10:00am-5:00pm. **U:** West Dulwich (BR) **B:** 12, 37, 38.

Twickenham, Richmond, and Hammersmith

Marble Hill House

Set in the center of a lovely park, Marble Hill House was built in 1724 as a summer home for Henrietta Howard, then mistress of King George II. While the Palladian-style mansion is handsome outside, the interior is splendid, embellished in white and gold with carved ornamentation, Ionic pillars, and fine ceiling decoration. The house also contains an excellent collection of Georgian paintings and furniture. *Address:* Richmond Rd., Twickenham (0181-892-5115). *Hours:* April-Sept: daily, 10:00am-6:00pm; Oct-March: 10:00am-4:00pm. **U:** Richmond. **B:** 33, 37, 90B, 202, 270, 290. **T**

Orleans House and Gallery

All that remains of the original Orleans House, where King Louis Phillipe (Duc d'Orleans) lived in exile from 1815 to 1817, is the unique Baroque Octagon. This masterpiece of architecture, designed by James Gibbs in 1719, today houses the Ionides Art Collection and the Richmond-Upon-Thames Art and Local History Collections. Few museums in London are better situated. *Address:* Riverside, Richmond Rd., Twickenham (0181-892-0221). *Hours:* Tues-Sat 1:00pm-5:30pm, Sun 2:00pm-5:30pm. **U:** Richmond. **B:** 33, 37, 90B, 202, 270, 290. **T**

Rugby Football Union Museum

Housed in National Stadium, this museum traces the history of rugby from its early 19th-century public school genesis to the contemporary international leagues. The free guided tour and film provide a thorough grounding in the sport for the uninitiated and veteran brawler alike. *Address:* Rugby Rd., Twickenham (0181-892-8161). *Hours:* Mon-Fri 9:30am-1:00pm & 2:00pm-5:00pm. **U:** Hounslow East. **B:** 281. **C T**

Royal Military School of Music Museum

The renowned 17th-century portrait painter Sir Godfrey Kneller built the mansion that now houses the Royal Army's music academy and museum. Music buffs are certain to enjoy the fine collection of historic instruments and other musical militaria. Free outdoor concerts and fireworks are presented during the summer. *Address:* Kneller Hall, Chertsey Rd., Twickenham (0181-898-5533). *Hours:* Mon, Tues, Thurs, & Fri 10:00am-noon & 2:00pm-4:00pm, Wed 10:00am-noon. **U:** Whitton (BR). **T**

Kew Public Records Office

National archives from the Norman conquest to the present are maintained by the Public Records Office. The modern Kew office has map and document reading rooms and provides instant information via computer terminals. *Address:* Ruskin Ave., Kew (0181-876-3444). *Hours:* Mon-Fri 9:30am-5:00pm. **U:** Kew Gardens. **B:** 27, 65. **H T**

Strawberry Hill

This fanciful Great House, built by Horace Walpole in 1770, was influential in the 18th- and 19th-century Gothic Revival movement. The towers, turrets, and battlements of Strawberry Hill now house St. Mary's College but are open for guided tours. Chief attractions in the "Castle" are the Tudor-style library, the Long Gallery, and the Banqueting Hall, resplendent with glittering chandeliers. *Address:* Waldegrave Rd., Twickenham (0181-892-0051). *Hours:* Wed & Sat 1:00pm-5:00pm (by appointment). **U:** St. Margaret's (BR). **B:** 33, 37, 90B, 202, 270. **T**

Kingston-Upon-Thames Heritage Centre

Opened in 1980, the Heritage Centre is a combined archaeological museum, art and photography gallery, archive, and regional history collection. A real highlight is the Muybridge Photographic Collection, based on the work of the motion picture pioneer. *Address:* Fairfield West, Kingston-Upon-Thames (0181-546-5386). *Hours:* Mon-Sat 10:00am-5:00pm. **U:** Kingston (BR). **B:** 111, 267. **H T**

Richmond Park

Richmond had been a royal hunting reserve for centuries when King Charles I enclosed 2,500 acres as a park in 1637. Britain's largest urban park still retains much of the atmosphere of a feudal manor, with ancient oaks, thorny thickets, bracken, plantation gardens, and wildlife. On a clear day, there are superb views of the Thames Valley from the top of Henry VIII's Mound — from St. Paul's Cathedral to Windsor Castle. *Address:* Kingston Vale, Richmond (0181-940-0654). *Hours:* daily, 7:00am to half-hour before dusk. **U:** Richmond. **B:** 72, 264. **H C**

Martinware Pottery Collection
Produced only in London by the Martin family from 1873 to 1923, Martinware is one of Britain's oddest forms of pottery. The Martins transformed salt-glazed stoneware into a fantastic variety of jugs, tea pots, animals, tiles, caricature pots, and architectural features. Their idiosyncratic work is now found in museums and galleries throughout the world. *Address:* Osterly Park Rd., Southall (0181-574-3412). *Hours:* Tues-Sat 9:00am-5:00pm. **U:** Southall (BR).

Guru Granth Gurdwara Temple
The Sikh religion plays a major role in the life of the London suburb of Southall. The friendly Guru Granth Gurdwara Temple is a great place to learn more about the religious sect. *Address:* 45 Villiers Rd., Southall (0181-574-7700). *Hours:* daily, 8:00am-8:00pm. **U:** Southall (BR).

Riverside Studios
First used as television studios by the BBC, Riverside Studios now constitutes a major arts complex, with galleries, theaters, workshops, and a cinema. There are frequent free exhibitions and special Saturday programs for children. *Address:* Crisp Rd., W6 (0181-741-2251). *Hours:* daily, noon-11:00pm. **U:** Hammersmith. **H C**

Hammersmith Local History Collection
This Borough of London history collection includes paintings, books, maps, photographs, and local memorabilia. *Address:* Shepherd's Bush Rd., W6 (0181-748-3020). *Hours:* Mon, Tues, Thurs, & Sat 9:15am-5:00pm. **U:** Hammersmith. **T**

Shepherd's Bush Market
There are strong Caribbean, African, and Indian influences at this colorful London market — a great place to find Asian tex-

tiles, Third World jewelry, and unusual foods. *Address:* Uxbridge & Goldhawk Rds., W12. *Hours:* Mon-Sat 9:00am-5:00pm. **U:** Shepherd's Bush, Goldhawk.

Kensal Green

Kensal Green is one of London's most interesting and eccentric Victorian cemeteries. Overgrown with ivy and brambles, it's an otherworldly retreat full of ornate tombs, lavish funerary monuments, and romantic statues. During the Victorian era, Kensal Green was *the* place to be interred. Celebrities buried there include William Makepeace Thackeray and Anthony Trollope. *Address:* Harrow Rd., W10 (0181-969-0152). *Hours:* Mon-Sat 9:00am-4:30pm. **U:** Kensal Green.

Outer Suburbs

Bruce Castle Museum

Dating from 1514, Bruce Castle has long served as the seat of the Lords of the Manor of Tottenham. Although a 16th-century tower remains, the Manor is mainly the result of 17th- and 18th-century additions and alterations. Today, it houses one of London's finest local history museums, with displays on domestic life in Haringey. There are also exhibits on colonial trade and the British postal system. A special attraction is the Museum of the "Diehards" Middlesex Regiment, who saw action against enemies of the Empire, from American Minutemen to Zulu warriors. *Address:* Lordship Lane, N17 (0181-808-8772). *Hours:* daily 1:00pm-5:00pm. **U:** Wood Green, Tottenham Hale. **B:** 243. **T**

Alexandra Park and Palace

Known to Londoners as "Ally Pally," Alexandra Palace is actually a gigantic Victorian exhibition center. The Palace once housed the BBC's first television studio, but today it's a multi-use entertainment complex. Surrounding the Palace, there's a 200-acre park with impressive views of London, a children's zoo and pool, a boating lake, mini-golf course, sports fields, playgrounds, and a bandstand for free concerts. Fairs, fireworks, and other special events are frequent attractions. *Address:* Wood Green, N22 (0181-365-2121 or 444-7696). *Hours:* open 24 hours. **U:** Wood Green. **B:** 144, 144A, W2, W3, W7. **H C**

London Museum of Jewish Life

This museum documents and illustrates Jewish social history in Great Britain. Displays include a reconstruction of a 19th-century tailor's workshop, photo exhibits, and a variety of religious and secular artifacts. *Address:* 80 East End Rd., N3 (0181-346-

2288). *Hours:* Mon-Thurs 10:00am-4:00pm, Sun 11:00am-5:00pm. **U:** Finchley Central. **T**

Golders Green Crematorium
Many of London's most important Jewish residents, including Sigmund Freud and rock star Marc Bolan, have memorials here. *Address:* Hoop Lane, NW11 (0181-455-2374). *Hours:* Mon-Fri 9:00am-5:00pm. **U:** Golders Green.

Pavlova Memorial Museum
Ivy House was the London home of the legendary ballerina Anna Pavlova from 1912 to her death in 1931. The touching museum has photographs, personal memorabilia, her touring trunk, a dressing table from the Palace Theatre, and ballet mementos. *Address:* North End Rd., NW11. *Hours:* Sat noon-5:00pm. **U:** Golders Green.

Church Farm House Museum
Built in 1659, the picturesque, gabled farmhouse is a rare example of a rapidly vanishing type of London home. This intriguing museum explores 17th- and 18th-century domestic life through period rooms and decorative art displays. Ask to see the attics, where original handmade tiles and thatch insulation are visible. The shady little garden in the back opens onto the meadows of Sunny Hill Park. *Address:* Greyhound Hill, NW4 (0181-203-0130). *Hours:* Mon, Wed, Sat 10:00am-5:30pm, Sun 2:00pm-5:30pm, Tues 10:00am-1:00pm. **U:** Hendon Central. **B:** 113, 143, 183. **T**

Newspaper Library Museum
Originating in 1762, the British Library's massive newspaper and periodical collection includes British dailies and weeklies, Commonwealth and colonial newspapers, plus such rarities as the *Matrimonial Post,* the 19th-century forerunner of today's "personals." *Address:* Colindale Ave., NW9 (0181-200-5515). *Hours:* Mon-Sat 10:00am-5:00pm. **U:** Colindale. **B:** 32, 226, 292. **T**

Grange Museum
Originally a stable in the late 1600's, the Grange Museum building today houses an engaging exhibition on the London borough of Brent and includes period rooms and a complete recon-

struction of an Edwardian draper's shop. There's also a special display on the 1924 British Empire Exhibition. *Address:* Neasden Lane, NW10 (0181-452-8311). *Hours:* Mon-Fri noon-5:00pm, Wed noon-7:00pm, Sat 10:00am-5:00pm. **U:** Neasden. **T**

Gunnersbury Park Museum

The Gunnersbury Park Museum is set in a lovely Regency mansion that was once a Rothschild family country estate. There are fine displays of local archaeological finds, antique means of transport, costumes, textiles, toys, a Victorian kitchen, and a contemporary art gallery. *Address:* Gunnersbury Park, Pope's Lane, W3 (0181-992-1612). *Hours:* March-Oct: Mon-Fri 1:00pm-5:00pm, Sat & Sun 2:00pm-6:00pm; Nov-Feb: daily 1:00pm-4:00pm. **U:** Acton Town. **H C T**

Hogarth's House

The famous artist and satirist William Hogarth lived in this "little country box by the Thames" from 1749 until his death in 1764. Now restored to its 18th-century condition, it presents a collection of Hogarth's paintings, prints, and engravings, plus personal memorabilia and period furnishings. *Address:* Hogarth Lane, Great West Road, W4 (0181-994-6757). *Hours:* April-August: Mon & Wed-Sat 11:00am-6:00pm, Sun 2:00pm-6:00pm; Sept-March: Mon & Wed-Sat 11:00am-4:00pm, Sun 2:00pm-4:00pm. **U:** Turnham Green. **B:** 290. **H T**

Epping Forest District Museum

Occupying two adjacent, 16th-century, timber-framed buildings, the Epping Museum explores the history of the Forest District from the Stone Age to the 20th century. Special loan displays from the Victoria and Albert Museum, along with the rural life collection and a charming Tudor herb garden, make this an especially diverting attraction. *Address:* 39 Sun St., Waltham Abbey, EN9 (0992-716882). *Hours:* Fri-Mon 2:00pm-5:00pm, Tues noon-5:00pm. **B:** 318, 333. **H T**

Lee Valley Park Countryside Centre

The Park Centre's aim is to help you make the most of your time in London's Lee Valley, with information on nearby sights like Hayes Hill Farm, Waltham Abbey Church, Dobbs Weir, and the notorious Rye House. It also presents a wide-ranging program of events on the ecology, history, and wildlife of the River Lee

Valley. *Address:* Crooked Mile, Waltham Abbey, EN9 (099-271-3838). *Hours:* daily, 10:00am-5:00pm. **H**

Waltham Abbey

Waltham Abbey, consecrated in 1066, is one of the finest surviving examples of Norman architecture in Britain. King Harold's corpse was brought to the Abbey after he was killed at the Battle of Hastings. A black marble slab is thought to be part of the King's sarcophagus. Despite 14th- and 19th-century alterations, the Abbey remains one of the most important monastic sites in the country. *Address:* Abbey Way, Waltham Abbey, EN9 (099-270-0766). *Hours:* daily, 10:00am-6:00pm. **B:** 318, 333.

Forty Hall Mansion

Forty Hall is a superb Caroline mansion built in 1629 for Sir Nicholas Raynton, a rich haberdasher and Lord Mayor of London. The ground floor rooms have elaborate Jacobean plaster ceilings and exceptional displays of 17th- and 18th-century furnishings. The upstairs is devoted primarily to an eccentric exhibit on the history of British advertising. There's also a nostalgic Victorian nursery and displays on the local ecology. The former stables are now gallery space for changing arts exhibitions. *Address:* Forty Hill, Enfield, EN2 (0181-363-8196). *Hours:* Tues-Sun 10:00am-6:00pm. **U:** Enfield Chase (BR). **B:** 191, 231. **H T**

Barnet Museum

London's Borough of Barnet Museum presents a wide-ranging collection that includes period costumes, scientific instruments, English decorative arts, and antiques. The real centerpiece of the museum, however, is a display exploring the Battle of Barnet in 1471, when Edward IV defeated the Earl of Warwick. *Address:* 31 Wood, EN5 (0181-449-0321). *Hours:* Tues-Thurs 2:30pm-4:30pm, Sat 10:00am-4:30pm. **U:** High Barnet.

Ford Motor Company

Ford's Dagenham plant has produced over 10 million cars and trucks since the first Model A left the line in 1931. The free tour lasts nearly two hours and covers two miles of behind-the-scenes views, so wear comfortable shoes. (You must make a reservation for the tour.) *Address:* New Road, Dagenham, RM8 (0181-592-3000). *Hours:* Mon-Fri 9:45am-4:00pm. **U:** Dagenham Heathway. **B:** 174, 175. **T**

Valence House

Aymer de Valence, Earl of Pembroke, built this moated, half-timbered manor house in the 14th century. Today it houses a museum of archaeological materials from the London area, including Stone and Iron Age tools, Roman artwork, and Anglo-Saxon jewelry, implements, and weapons. *Address:* Becontree Ave., Dagenham, RM8 (0181-592-2211). *Hours:* Mon-Fri 10:00am-4:00pm. **U:** Becontree. **T**

Kodak Museum

The Kodak Museum presents exhibits covering the history of photography and cinematography from the 19th century to the modern era of satellite reconnaissance. Special features include a restored Victorian photo studio and a multi-projector audiovisual show. *Address:* Headstone Drive, Harrow (0181-863-0534). *Hours:* Mon-Fri 9:30am-4:30pm, Sat & Sun 2:00pm-6:00pm. **U:** Harrow & Wealdstone (BR). **B:** H1. **C**

Harrow Heritage Centre

Opened in 1986, the Harrow Heritage Centre is designed to promote Harrow's lesser known attractions. Housed in an old tithe barn, the Centre presents changing exhibitions on the history, crafts, lifestyles, and ecology of the area, plus open-air entertainment during the summer. *Address:* Headstone Lane, Harrow (0181-861-2626). *Hours:* Tues-Fri noon-4:00pm, Sat & Sun 10:30am-5:00pm. **U:** Headstone (BR). **C**

Public Record Office Museum

Housed in an ornate neo-Gothic building, this museum presents an illustrious selection of British documents dating to the Norman conquest. Outstanding national treasures on display include the Domesday Book of 1086, the Magna Charta, Shakespeare's will, *H.M.S. Victory's* log, royal correspondence, and the "Olive Branch Petition" from the nascent U.S. Congress to King George III. *Address:* Ruskin Ave., Kew TW9 (0181-876-3444). *Hours:* Mon-Fri 9:30am-5:00pm. **U:** Kew Gardens. **B:** 27, 65. **T H** (call first)

Radio London

BBC fans won't want to miss an opportunity to be in the audience for one of BBC Radio's live shows. Free tickets are usually available for quiz shows, interview programs, and classical concerts. The studio is located in lovely Maida Vale at Delaware Rd., W9, but first contact BBC Radio Ticket Unit at 0171-765-5243. **U:** Maida Vale.

Afro-British Arts

Yaa Asantewaa Arts Centre is the hub of African and Caribbean arts and culture in northwest London. Daily activities range from craft exhibitions and art shows to dance performances and workshops. Hours: daily 11:00am-7:00pm. Address: 1 Chipping Mews W9 (0171-286-1656). **U:** Warwick Ave., Maida Vale, Royal Oak.

Annual Free Events

January

1st—*Lord Mayor of Westminster's New Year's Day Parade.* The parade starts at 1:00pm from Piccadilly Circus, continues through Regent Street and Oxford Street, and finishes in Hyde Park. There will be marching bands from around the world, colorful floats, and thousands of dancers and marchers from all over the UK. Throughout the day, a variety of performances run in Hyde Park, and a spectacular fireworks display culminates the festivities.

Last Sunday—*Charles I Commemoration.* On January 30, 1649, King Charles I was executed. This event is commemorated on the last Sunday in January each year by the "King's Army," dressed and armed in authentic 17th-century style. The march begins at St. James's Palace at 11:30am and makes its way down the Mall, through Horse Guards, to the Banqueting House, following the route of the King's last walk. A ceremony is held at the scaffold site, followed by Commissioning of Officers. The parade then marches to the Trafalgar Square statue of Charles I, through the Admiralty Arch, and back down the Mall to St. James's Palace.

February

Chinese New Year—Usually celebrated on the first or second Sunday of February, the New Year's festival is the annual highlight of London's Chinese community. The area of Soho's Chinatown, around Newport Place, Gerrard St., and Lisle St., comes alive with streamers, decorations, and garlands. Lion and dragon dancers weave through the crowds of revelers, craft displays, food stalls, and fireworks. There's also a performance stage in nearby Leicester Square.

First Sunday — *Clown's Service.* This unique and colorful event occurs at Holy Trinity Church, Beechwood Road, E8. Members of Clowns International in full make-up and costume attend the annual 2:00pm service and perform afterwards in the church hall.

March

Spring Equinox — *Druid Ceremony.* At noon on the vernal equinox, Druids in hooded gowns gather at Tower Hill Terrace to celebrate the season with ancient symbolic rites.

Last Saturday — *Head of the River Race.* This race, from Mortlake to Putney, is a processional race for eight-man shells. Starting at 10-second intervals, 420 crews compete for the fastest time. The best viewpoint is from the Surrey bank above Chiswick Bridge.

April

Easter Sunday — *Easter Parade.* Each year, thousands flock to Battersea Park for one of London's biggest events. The parade starts at 1:00pm with brightly colored floats, marching bands, samba dancers, and costumed characters circumnavigating the park's perimeter. Other entertainment and attractions include a fair, jazz concert, children's theater, and steel band.

Easter Monday — *Harness Horse Parade.* This Regent's Park event salutes London's working horses in a unique competition for prizes of rosettes and brass merit badges. The program begins at 9:30am at the Inner Circle and climaxes at noon with the Grand Parade.

21st — *Queen's Birthday Salute.* There's an exciting 41-gun salute at noon in Green Park each year to celebrate the Queen's birthday. Pulling massive gun carriages, the King's Troop of the Royal Horse Artillery gallops through the park, sets up, and fires.

All month — *Camden Festival.* A month-long celebration of music and art occurs throughout the Borough of Camden. For details, call 071-278-4444.

May

1st — *May Day Celebration.* Annual Labour Party processional to Hyde Park.

Ascension Day — *Beating the Bounds.* For centuries the boundaries of each London parish were reaffirmed by an annual ceremony. Although few parishes retain the event, a colorful ceremony still occurs each year at All Hallows by the Tower. At 1:00pm, choirboys with willow wands vigorously beat the boundaries around the Tower of London, including one in mid-Thames. The public is welcome to join the procession.

2nd through 14th — *Victoria Embankment Art Exhibition.* Annual open-air art show along the Thames at Victoria Embankment.

29th — *Oak-Apple Day.* Traditional parade and ceremonies at the Royal Hospital Chelsea.

Last weekend — *Spring Bank Holiday Fairs.* Annual fairs are held during the holiday weekend at Alexandra Park, Hampstead Heath, and Battersea Park.

June

2nd Saturday — *Trooping the Colour.* This ceremony celebrates the Queen's "official birthday." The Queen leaves Buckingham Palace at 10:40am in an open coach and proceeds down the

Mall to Horse Guards, arriving at 11:00am. As the Queen arrives, the band plays the national anthem and an honor guard fires a gun salute. After reviewing the parade, the Queen returns to the palace for a Royal Air Force fly-by at 1:00pm.

24th — *Presentation of the Rose.* In a ceremony at the Mansion House dating to the 14th century, a freshly plucked rose is presented by a descendant of Lord Knollys to the Lord Mayor of London.

24th — *Sheriffs of the City Election.* The Lord Mayor and Alderman take part in this colorful, ancient ceremony at the Guildhall.

Mid-month — *Greenwich Festival.* Cultural and entertainment events at venues around the Borough and in Greenwich Park. For details, call 0181-854-8888.

Weekends — *Hampstead Open-Air Art Exhibition.* The Hampstead Arts Council sponsors this annual show on Hampstead Heath.

Late June — *City of London Festival.* City halls, churches, and museums are the locales for non-stop entertainment. Call 0171-248-4260 for details.

July

2nd Wednesday — *Vintner's Company Road Sweeping Procession.* After the swearing-in of the new master of the Vintner's Guild, a costumed procession goes from the Company Hall on Upper Thames Street to the church of St. James Garlichythe. It's headed by the Company's Tackle Porters in top hats and white smocks, who sweep the road so the Company Master can pass unhindered. The traditional ceremonies date back to 1327.

Mid-month — *Doggett's Coat and Badge Race.* This famous river race from London Bridge to Chelsea for single sculls was founded in 1715 by Thomas Doggett to celebrate the accession of King George I. The popular actor established a trust to award a silver badge and scarlet coat to the race winner. The best views are from London Bridge, where the race begins at 6:45pm.

Mid-month — *Clerkenwell Festival.* Street performances, concerts, and events in sites around Clerkenwell and Islington. For details, call 0171-354-7127 or 0171-226-3640.

August

1st Sunday — *Riding Horse Parade.* Commencing at 1:00pm in Hyde Park, this competition selects the best turned-out London horse and rider. The "Supreme Champion" receives the Astral Sports Perpetual Challenge Cup.

First week — *Summer in the City.* A family-oriented festival of arts and entertainment, organized by the Barbican Centre.

Third weekend — *Asian Festival.* Lambeth Council sponsors this fascinating celebration of Asian culture at the charming Rookery on Streatham Common. You can expect lots of music, dance, crafts, food, and children's activities.

Bank Holiday — *Notting Hill Carnival.* Established in 1965 as a children's carnival, Notting Hill has become Europe's largest street festival. Revelers sing and dance around Portobello Road and Ladbroke Grove to reggae bands, brass bands, steel bands, and outdoor discos. Other attractions are colorful floats, spectacular Caribbean costumes, live entertainment, and tons of West Indian food. For two weeks beforehand, there are daily pre-Carnival events at the Carnival Village in Wormwood Scrubs Park. For details, call 0181-964-0544.

Bank Holiday — *Hampstead Holiday Fair.* Annual fair complete with cotton candy and amusement park rides held on Hampstead Heath, North End.

September

First Saturday — *Thamesday*. Day-long party in Jubilee Gardens, South Bank to celebrate London's river. The diverse program of events includes craft exhibits, street performers, ethnic food, "Green" activities, a funfair, and races — all culminating with evening fireworks on the Thames.

Second week — *Battle of Britain Week*. Week-long series of memorials, RAF fly-bys, and remembrance services at Westminster Abbey and other London churches.

Second week — *International Covent Garden Festival*. A 10-day extravaganza of performing arts from around the world. For details, call 0171-497-8903.

Last Sunday — *Chinatown Autumn Festival*. Mini version of the colorful Chinese New Year celebration with dragon dances, street entertainment, and plenty of food.

Michaelmas Day — *Election of the Lord Mayor of London*. Centuries-old traditional ceremonies are held at the Mansion House, Guildhall, and St. Lawrence-Jewry Church.

October

First Sunday — *Costermonger's Pearly Harvest Festival*. A Trafalgar Square celebration of the cockney tradition of the Pearly Kings and Queens. Hundreds of produce sellers assemble at St. Martin-in-the-Fields in marvelous costumes covered in mother-of-pearl buttons.

21st — *Trafalgar Day Parade*. The anniversary of Lord Nelson's historic sea victory at the Battle of Trafalgar is commemorated annually by a parade and service. Hundreds of Sea Cadets from all over the UK, along with marching bands, parade through the square and lay wreaths at the foot of Nelson's Column.

November

First Sunday — *London to Brighton Veteran Car Run.* This unique rally — only cars built before 1905 can enter — attracts over 400 entrants from around the world. The run began in 1896 when the law compelling motorists to have a man carrying a red flag walking in front of them was abolished. Arrive at Hyde Park by 8:00am for the start.

5th — *Fireworks Night.* Fireworks displays and huge bonfires in parks celebrate the arrest of Guy Fawkes and his co-conspirators in the 1605 plot to blow-up Parliament. Effigies of the "Guy" are tossed on bonfires for the finale.

Second Saturday — *Lord Mayor's Show.* The tradition of the Lord Mayor's Show, when he rides in his gilded, 18th-century coach to the Law Courts for the declaration of office, dates from the 13th century. Hundreds of colorful floats, military bands, and marching units accompany the plume-hatted mayor. The two-hour processional begins at St. Lawrence-Jewry at 11:00am and snakes through the old City streets, winding up at the Mansion House.

Second Sunday — *Remembrance Sunday.* The Cenotaph Memorial at Whitehall is the scene of the annual memorial service for Commonwealth citizens who lost their lives in the two World Wars. Detachments of the Army and Navy, along with ex-servicemen and -women, assemble at 10:00am for band music while awaiting the arrival of the Queen at 10:59am. A two-minute silence is heralded and ended by a cannon salute, after which the Last Post is sounded by Royal Marine buglers, and the Queen lays a wreath at the Cenotaph.

Mid-month — *State Opening of Parliament.* You can view the Royal Procession of the Queen and Crown in the Irish or Australian State Coach on the route along the Mall through Horse Guards Parade, Whitehall, and Parliament Square. They depart Buckingham Palace at 10:37am, and the Royal Horse Artillery in Hyde Park fires a 41-gun salute at 11:15am as the Queen arrives at the Sovereign's Entrance to the House of Lords. Phone 0171-219-3107 for exact date.

The State Opening of Parliament in November. (BTA photo)

December

6th — *Christmas Tree.* Since 1947, the City of Oslo has presented a Norwegian spruce Christmas tree as an expression of gratitude for Britain's help in WWII. The tree is erected in Trafalgar Square and decorated with Norwegian-style lights. Carolers sing around the tree each night until Christmas Eve.

31st — *New Year's Eve Celebration.* Massive crowds gather around Nelson's Column in Trafalgar Square to ring in the New Year with singing, dancing, and a general, good-natured, British "knees-up."

More Great Books
from Mustang Publishing

Europe for Free by Brian Butler. If you're on a tight budget—
or if you just love a bargain—this is the book for you! With
descriptions of thousands of things to do and see for free all
over Europe, you'll save plenty of lira, francs, and shillings.
$10.95

*"Forget about American Express. One of these books is
what you shouldn't leave home without!"*—Toronto Sun

Also in this series:
Hawaii for Free by Frances Carter. **$9.95**
Paris for Free (Or Extremely Cheap) by Mark Beffart. **$10.95**
The Southwest for Free by Greg & Mary Jane Edwards. **$9.95**
DC for Free by Brian Butler. **$9.95**

Northern Italy: A Taste of Trattoria by Christina Baglivi. For
the most delicious, most authentic, and least expensive
meals in Italy, skip the *ristoranti* and head straight to *trattorie*,
the small, unassuming cafés known only to locals. With over
80 *trattorie* from Rome to Milan, it's a must for the hungry
traveler. **$12.95**

*"The book's general premise is as sound as its
specific eatery recommendations."*—N.Y. Daily News

How to Be a Way Cool Grandfather by Verne Steen. Some
things a grandfather just *ought* to know: how to make a
slingshot from an old limb and a rubber band, how to make
a kite from a newspaper, how to do a few simple magic
tricks, and how to make his grandchildren say, "Cool,
Grandpa!" With complete details on making 30 fun, inexpensive toys, plus hints on using them to impart valuable les-
sons to kids, this is a great book for every old fogey who'd
rather be way cool. **$12.95**

"A charming book."—The Spokesman-Review

101 Classic Jewish Jokes by Robert Menchin. From the Borscht Belt shtick of Rodney Dangerfield to the urbane wit of Jerry Seinfeld, Jewish humor has had a huge influence on modern comedy. With 101 classic jokes, plus witty drawings and hilarious trivia, this book is a must for fans of Jewish humor—or anyone who needs a good laugh! **$9.95**
"A hilarious compendium!"—Midwest Book Review

The Complete Book of Golf Games by Scott Johnston. Want to spice up your next round of golf? With over 80 great betting games, side wagers, and tournament formats, this book will delight both weekend hackers and the totally obsessed. From descriptions of favorite games like Skins and Nassau to details on unusual contests like String and Bingo Bango Bongo, it's essential equipment in every golfer's bag. **$12.00**
"Entertaining and informative"—Petersen's Golfing

The Complete Book of Beer Drinking Games by Griscom, Rand, & Johnston. With over 500,000 copies sold, this book reigns as the imbiber's bible! From classic games like Quarters and Blow Pong to wild new creations like Slush Fund and Beer Hunter—plus numerous funny essays, cartoons, and lists—this book is a party essential! **$8.95**
"The 'Animal House' of literature!"—Dallas Morning News

Mustang books should be available at your local bookstore. If not, send a check or money order for the price of the book, plus $3.00 shipping *per book,* to Mustang Publishing, P.O. Box 770426, Memphis, TN 38177 U.S.A. To order by credit card, call toll-free 800-250-8713 or 901-684-1200.

Allow two weeks for delivery. For rush, three-day delivery, add $2.00 to the total. *International orders:* Please pay in U.S. funds, and add $5.00 per book for Air Mail.

For a complete catalog of Mustang books, send $2.00 and a stamped, self-addressed, business-size envelope to Catalog Request, Mustang Publishing, P.O. Box 770426, Memphis, TN 38177 U.S.A.